Sidebar:
A Sideways Look
At the Lawyer's Life

M.C. Bruce

ISBN:
ISBN-478-304-96015-3

DEDICATION

To Dean, Debbie, Ron, Don, Sheryl, Sharon, Dave D., Tom, Carl
and all the other Public Defenders
who had the misfortune of supervising me over the years.

Contents

M.C. Bruce

Two Lawyers Walk Into the Bar:
Why Lawyers Are Not Funny

It is a widely known fact that when a lawyer tells a joke, someone loses his house.

Lawyers are not funny. Not even a little bit. This was brought home during the recent Florida trial during which a defense lawyer, opening his case, told what he believed to be a joke and the jury stared back at him as if he'd just pulled his pants down in the courtroom. What was actually funny was the startled expression on the lawyer's face when he realized that no one was laughing. I'm sure the joke had killed back at the law firm but then, most of those people probably thought they were being paid to laugh at the man's jokes.

Lawyers are not funny. If you have ever tried to read a so-called humor column in any local bar association paper, you will notice that the column sounds more like a Supreme Court brief than a Mark Twain essay. It is usually filled with words like *res ipsa loquitor* and citations to *Pennoyer v. Neff1*. There are footnotes. When was the last time you laughed at a footnote?

Lawyers are not funny, even though in their hearts every lawyer wants two things: To be the hero of a John Grisham novel, and to be a standup comedian. But when your jokes start with "So the party of the first part says to the party of the second part..." –you are just not going to kill the room.

Lawyers are not funny, and I myself am proving it by

---

1 95 U.S. 714. Try that out at your next cocktail party.

repeating that line over and over again, as if I am trying to develop some kind of comedic theme which might eventually get you to laugh at the absurdity of dark birds of prey in expensive suits thinking they are each a courtroom Robin Williams. But let's face it: There's a reason why, in his varied career roles, Robin Williams has never played a lawyer.

This is especially peculiar when you realize that in other areas of literature—okay, one area of literature, the legal thriller—lawyer writers are all the rage. John Grisham. Steve Margolis. Scott Turow. They write pretty good books, they sell millions, and every damned one of them quits the law as quickly as they can to pursue the muse.

But reading any one of these and a thousand other lawyer authors will instantly tell you why they succeed in courtroom drama and fail at literary pies in the face. The courtroom drama revolves around a trusty formula: A beautiful or handsome trial lawyer is given the case of his or her life and then discovers he/she is falling in love with his/her client or the opposing lawyer or some street urchin who turns out to be an heiress. There's usually a lot of very dull sex, described as you would read it in an indictment for forcible oral copulation, and then an exciting courtroom scene in which the cross examination of the handsome/beautiful lawyer reveals the ugly truth to all concerned. Then the handsome/beautiful lawyer quits the law firm/District Attorney's Office and either goes out on their own or buys a farm out in Vermont where they can grow dandelions. The end. Or is it?

Lawyers are happy to write formula. Hell, it's what we do every time we sit down to write a motion or a writ or a brief on appeal. There are structures that we dare not tamper with. Were we to get creative with anything, we would hear about it from the judge, who will make a snarky comment about our writing style, thinking he is funny and probably wondering whether he should start collecting his better bon mots for a book of judicial wit and wisdom.

But comedy is about breaking formula. Comedy is about the unexpected. Comedy is quick and sharp and somewhat mean spirited. The only thing the lawyers can usually manage is the mean spirited part.

The problem is that a lawyer's training is antithical to funny. In our lives it is the calm, plodding reasoned argument which is the most successful. In law school we are pounded into submission by the Socratic method, which pins us to the chair with unanswerable questions about cases and laws and reasoning and why did the judge grant this motion when clearly the equity was on the other side. We learn in law school to suspect emotion, to fear the unexpected, to shun the original. We argue from past case law, statutes, law reviews. Which, in turn, rely on past case law, statutes and law reviews. Which, in turn, relied on that guy Blackstone, who wrote several volumes of legal analysis and not a chicken crossing the road comment in any of them.

So when lawyers go into real life, and they see the dworky guy with the minimum wage job getting the gorgeous girls because he tells good jokes. They think: "Hey, that would work on a jury." Or they think they can write a humor piece that will get all the other lawyers laughing with them.

(For one moment, think of the sound of a group of lawyers laughing. If that doesn't send a chill down your spine, nothing will.)

In truth, law school is designed to iron out every creative and humanistic impulse in your being. I learned this early in my first semester. Before becoming a lawyer, I had some moderate success as a stand-up comedian in the Air Force and in civilian life. At least, I could make people laugh if they were drunk enough (not usually a problem on Air Force bases). So when we began to study *Christian v. Rowland2* and the instructor said in a conspiratorial tone

---

2 69 Cal. 2d 108 (1968). Is it me or is that a somewhat salacious citation for a case involving a pair of lovers?

that the injured plaintiff who was an invitee on the property was probably Rowland's lover, I belted out the following to the tune of *Frankie and Johnny:*

> *Christian and Rowland were lovers.*
> *Oh, Lordy, how they could love.*
> *But Christian got injured in Rowland's apartment*
> *And they gave the law a shove.*
> *He was the plaintiff*
> *But she done him wrong.*

The instructor looked at me as if I were mad. The rest of the class rolled their eyes. No one wanted to join in my musical while there were important legal premises to be diced and sliced so that they could get high paying jobs at law firms.

Of course, looking at the thing now, it's actually pathetic that I even thought the song was funny. It's typical lawyer humor. It's only missing the footnote.

After three years at Boalt Hall, I staggered forth into the world and tried my damnedest to become a somber, unfunny counselor of the law. But I made a big mistake. I became a Public Defender, a job which seemed to be calculated to give me a sardonic view of life. When I went to tell one client that he shouldn't take his shoplifting case to trial because there was videotape of him taking the stuff, he looked me in the eye and said "The videotape is lying."

And I'm supposed to remain somber after that?

Even after I went solo for five long years, I seemed to be afflicted with a sense of humor. When one opponent at a deposition implied I was trying to trick him (I wasn't but he was very obnoxious), he yelled at me, "I'm not as dumb as I look." I, unfortunately, responded, "That wouldn't be possible."

So from time to time I wrote a little essay on the vagaries of the law, many of which have been published under the name "Sidebar." I didn't choose the title. A non-lawyer editor did. Which is why it's so punchy.

The columns actually made lawyers laugh. Non-lawyers, too. A few of the columns were reprinted in various bar journals. The California State Bar even used a few in their instructional materials, usually as cautionary tales about what would happen to your lawyer's brain if you tried to be funny. It got so ridiculous in the San Fernando Valley that some fool nominated me for a seat on the SFVBA Board of Directors, a position for which I did not campaign and which I won handily. Joke was on them, though. I went back to work in Orange County for the Public Defender and never served. Ha!

In my capacity as court jester to two different bar associations (the OCBA ran about 10 of my columns before the Board told them "we aren't running a humor magazine"), I was privy to reading other lawyers' works of alleged wit. To a person they were long, tedious recitations of case law and tired jokes. It made me worry. Was I like that, too?

I still don't know, my friends. Seems to me that funny is like poetry. You either got it or you don't, but you always think the best and worst of your own work. And if you have the lawyer's ego, you are constantly telling yourself how great you are and reminding yourself that you ain't that great after all. Unfortunately, when one writes a funny piece (or what one hopes is a funny piece), there is no judge to submit a ruling.3

Lawyers, my friends, are not funny. Their clients, on the other hand, are hysterical.

---

3 And the fact that I'm using the passive third person in this sentence bothers me as much as it does you.

THE VAGARIES OF THE LAW

The law has ruined my life.

I used to have friends. I used to have a family life. I used to come home before dark. I was able to watch *Perry Mason* without shouting objections at the tube.

All of that changed the day I passed the bar. My friends and family noticed the difference, and commented unkindly upon it. They figured that, being a lawyer, I naturally had thick skin.

My little sister told me that she could never tell me a story about her kids without suffering a cross-examination from me. She said I would even shout (over the telephone, no less), "I don't want you to explain yourself, just answer the question 'Yes' or 'No.'"

My brother told me that every time he told me that latest joke about Madonna that I would lecture him on libel and explain what damages she would collect against him. (To date, Madonna has seen fit to keep my brother out of court.)

My friend Leslie told me that whenever she told me something that happened to a mutual friend, I would treat it like a bar exam hypothetical question. She says she got tired of me asking, "But where's the tort?"

The law has ruined my life. I can't seem to walk around my house now without looking for pockets of liability. When driving my car, if I narrowly avoid an accident, I no longer breathe a sigh of relief; I analyze who would have been at fault if we *had* collided. Whenever I read a newspaper article, I keep scanning ahead to see what the "holding" is.

The law has ruined my life. People avoid me at parties because they are afraid to get into arguments with me. The only people who will talk to me are those who collect lawyer jokes. No one laughs at my doctor jokes.

The law has ruined my life. My parenting partner knows better now than to ask me how my day went. My family knows better than to call and ask me legal advice. My friends have given up on the idea that I will ever be a normal, tolerable human being.

I liken it to the old idea that the law sometimes does incomprehensible things due to perfectly flawless legal reasoning. One judge called it, "The vagaries of the law." As lawyers, we often experience the incomprehensible. Hey, sometimes we *create* the incomprehensible ---all with perfect legal reasoning. The unfortunate thing is, we carry the vagaries of the law into our private lives, our dealings with clients, our dealings with each other.

Despite the fact that we become irrationally abusive to each other when booming broadsides at each other during litigation, in the end we all sail in the same boat. It is one of the vagaries of the law that the law has ruined our lives -- yet it's incomprehensible that we would have chosen any other profession.

MEMO TO MR. CRUISE

Memo to Tom Cruise: Cut it out.

You know what I'm talking about, Tom. First you play a handsome, sexy young lawyer who cares deeply and passionately about his clients in "A Few Good Men." Then you play a handsome, sexy young lawyer with a passion for righting wrongs and jumping out of windows in "The Firm." Now your buddy Julia Roberts (you movie stars are all buddies, aren't you?) is going to play a beautiful, sexy young law student who cares passionately about justice in "The Pelican Brief."

I don't know if you quite understand the damage you're doing to my practice. I can see it in a client's eyes when they first meet me: They've been expecting a muscled, blue-eyed hunk of a lawyer. Instead there's this chubby teddy bear extending a paw in greeting.

Their disappointments mount. In your movies, Tom, seems like all you have to do with your time is concentrate on one client's case. In a just cause, you spend nights and weekends doing every ounce of research, investigation, ratiocination on the zealous search for truth.

My clients call me and find out I'm in court on another matter. Or I'm talking to another client. Or I'm (heaven forbid) out to lunch with a friend. Hey, where's this zealous pursuit of justice? It doesn't matter that their case is months away from seeing a courtroom; time's a wasting.

The topper, Tom, is the way you and your movie lawyer friends always pull the rabbit out of the hat. In "A Few Good Men," you get Jack Nicholson to admit that he condoned an illegal order by badgering him on the witness stand. Your brilliant cross-examination goes like this: "I want the truth."

When we go to court, my client fully expects me to

badger each witness, accusing them of lying if they utter a word against our case. They expect me to shout at them "I want the truth."

Hey, Tom, I might as well shout, "I want to be found in contempt! And take my bar card while you're at it!"

My clients are disgruntled, Tom. I don't look like a lawyer. I don't obsessively work like a lawyer. I don't shout in court like a lawyer. No wonder they're so reluctant to pay my fees--even when I win.

Look Tom, you can take any role you want, but I have to be a lawyer for the rest of my natural life. I know I do. They keep rejecting me at plumbing school.

Play a doctor. Play a golfer. Play a garage mechanic. These guys won't suffer when you look more heroic than they. Nobody's going to look up at their chubby doctor before heart surgery and say, "Do it like Cruise does it in the movies, doc."

Or, if you must play a lawyer, do me a favor: Put on some weight. Growl at your client about unpaid fees. And try to manage to lose a case once in a while. It'll make my clients feel a whole lot better.

Thanks for your anticipated cooperation.

P.S. Can you get me Kim Basinger's telephone number? I've got this script about this gorgeous witness who gets involved with a chubby lawyer....

THE DEFAULT ZONE

Somewhere deep in the wilds of Superior Court is a mysterious place where cases go but never return. For ages it has lain undiscovered, shrouded in the thickets of the clerk's office. Some say that if you could wander through this place, the bleached bones of once viable litigation would block your way. Others say no, that the missing lawsuits are perfectly preserved, frozen in time for some undisclosed later released from suspended animation.

It is the Default Zone, and woe to the attorney whose case innocently wanders into it.

I will play the Ancient Mariner in this tale, an albatross of a Wrongful Termination suit hung about my neck. Allow me to pluck you on the sleeve on your way to the feast--or your status conference--and tell you a tale of woe.

Oh, it was a good enough case. The law seemed to be on my client's side. His declaration was loving and gentle. I even looked in the local court rules a few months after the employer failed to answer our ringing complaint, so that I could submit the default papers correctly.

The client was excited. To win without even a trial! Did I warn him? Caution him? Send him to the oracle for advice? No, arrogant fool attorney that I was, the default would be easy!

A month after we submitted the papers to the default clerk I received a packet back. The judgment! I exulted.

But against the rocks of the unofficial, unpromulgated rules, my hopes were dashed. "This packet requires a statement regarding damages," it said. But I *had* submitted that at the time of the default request. And the court rules said nothing about this "requirement."

14

Oh, well, I told the client. We'll try again with their precious statement. It was only a month to wait.

But now the default clerks smelled drawn blood. The papers were returned again a month later--I'd calculated the interest wrong, she said. I called and screamed at her, but she was unmoved. I would have to calculate the damages and the interest month by month.

Thus began my descent into the default maelstrom. A month later the default was rejected because the client's declaration was wrong. A month later it was a missing form generated only by this default clerk's office. A month later it was rejected because last month's form was no longer in use-- and, by the way, the damages had to be recalculated.

From this delirium of default there is no rest, no refuge, no resolution. Judges scorn my motions to go over the clerks' heads, and the clerks, newly enraged, comb my papers for errant commas and misplaced vowels.

I have become a fixture at the default offices, begging clerks to tell me how to fix the case. Yea, and I am only one of a host of the lost lawyers, the glassy eyed stare of default in our eyes.

So, stranger, heed my warning. Beg your opponents to answer your complaints. Save yourself from my fate.

And one last request: Will you sign this substitution of attorney for me?

ATTORNEY GUILT

There are old jokes about Jewish guilt and Catholic guilt (the best of which a Jewish friend of mine told me: "You Catholics feel guilt because you answer to God; we Jews have a much heavier guilt--we answer to our mothers.") No one has ever explored the most powerful, most motivating, the ugliest guilt of all:

Attorney Guilt.

You know the kind. You're home on a weekend trying to enjoy a football game. The back of your mind keeps digging at you for not researching that Motion to Compel due next Friday.

Or you work for a big law firm and you wander out the door at 7 P.M. You duck past the doors of partners who are still there and working--and will be until 10:00.

Or you're standing in court for a motion and the Judge cites to you an obscure case from Rhode Island. You sink inwardly with shame for not having done a 50 state search on the issue.

The guilt starts in law school, during the second week of classes. You're so filled with hope and arrogance that you fail to notice that the people around you are just as smart or smarter. The guy next to you is called on to recite in class, and he begins to analogize the case to other cases The footnotes! My Lord, who reads cases listed in the footnotes? Is this guy a whacko?

Then you note the satisfied grin on your professor's face and you realize that *you* should have read the cases in the footnotes. What kind of lousy, lazy student are you, anyway?

From that moment on, the law haunts your life. You study for the bar and refuse to take a weekend off for fear of missing an important part of Civil Procedure on the test. You start working as a young associate and find yourself distracted on a date with a woman because there are depositions that need summarizing.

You are not alone.

As attorneys, we not only value the workaholics, we idolize them. The rest of the world laughed when it discovered Richard Nixon's lawyer's nickname was "Old Iron Butt." We knew it was a term of awe.

The journals pointed at the modern lawyer also perpetuate our guilt. One month we see, on the cover of *California Lawyer,* a picture of a powerful woman lawyer who eats, sleeps and breathes products liability. The magazine calls her the "Woman's Warrior." We see this and feel a twinge of guilt--who have we rescued in the law lately? Maybe we should treat our clients nicer when they call. Maybe we should do more pro bono. Maybe we've been spending too much time with the family and not enough time at work.

Guilt is a powerful feeling. It's more insidious than addiction; more debilitating than depression.

Without guilt, we'd have to live a 9 to 5 life. We'd have to admit that we were normal.

Heaven forbid. Like the White Rabbit, we lawyers are constantly on the go from one half-finished job to another. Is the law library open this late? We're attorneys and, needless to say, our work is never done.

It could be worse, though; we could have to answer to our mothers.

SUGGESTIONS FOR A LIVELY PRACTICE

Attorneys are a dull lot. Imagination in an attorney is often viewed with suspicion and alarm. No wonder our favorite suit colors--both men and women--are gray and dark blue.

It's time to stop this foolishness. For those who want to help me spice up the dull image of attorneys, here are some suggestions to help liven up your practice:

* On your next criminal case, pull out a boom box and do your final argument in Rap:

> *I'm the lawyer man*
> *and I'm here to say*
> *You gotta let my client*
> *walk today.*
> *The D.A. man*
> *don't have a case.*
> *So let my man*
> *Outa this bad place--break it out!*

* When you're interviewing a prospective client who's whining about his last attorney--so you know you're not going to take the case anyway--spin around in your chair, put your fingers in your ears and start humming "I can't hear you, la la la."

* When opposing counsel is on the phone lying about why he hasn't produced discovery, pretend you're Howard Stern and start grilling him on his sex life.

* When in trial, if the judge keeps making wacky rulings against you, turn to the opposing attorney and say,

loud enough for the jury to hear you, "Mom always did like you best."

    * When you win a motion, spike your briefcase on the counsel table like a football and high five your client.

    * When the other attorney tries to make excuses to get out of sanctions, whine like a puppy or squawk like a chicken.

    * When calling a client for a long-overdue bill, act like you've been interrupted and say, loud enough for the telephone receiver to pick up, "Tell Don Corleone I may ask him to return the favor very soon."

    * Leave your secretary alone for a week. Watch her go crazy.

    * Start using "Did not" as your major cross-examination tactic.

    * Start telling surly courtroom clerks that your client is a war vet who hates bureaucrats and could snap at any minute. Tell your client to stare at the clerk without blinking.

    * While the D.A. is cross examining your client, start the drum solo to "In a Gadda Da Vida" softly on your briefcase, so that only the D.A. can hear it. Act innocent when she complains to the judge.

    * Tell insurance adjusters on Personal Injury cases that you know where they live, you've got a box of eggs and you're not afraid to use them.

    * When a witness at a deposition starts to answer every question with "I don't remember," start referring to him as "Mr. Reagan."

    * End every opposition to Summary Judgment with the idea that the earth will explode in 2 billion years and nothing the court does can stop it.

    * Instead of citing cases in a reply brief, give the court the Top Ten Reasons Opposing Counsel is a Geek.

    * Renew your malpractice insurance.

THE GRATITUDE OF CLIENTS

A client has the gratitude of a cat.
A cat will allow you to stroke its fur because a cat enjoys it. A cat will rub itself lovingly against your legs and meow hopefully until you trip over it and break your neck--or you feed it. As long as you're useful to the cat, it will be faithful to you.

But the moment there's trouble, it's every hairy beast for itself. You just don't hear about a cat dragging its unconscious owner from a flaming house, or attacking an intruder with claw and tooth to protect its master.

Cats and clients are two of a kind. When the client first comes to you, he or she is distraught, emotional, angry, scared. You are the powerful god of law who will descend to bring wrongdoers to justice.

But don't be mislead by the client's effusive expressions of gratitude. They may slobber all over you like a dog, but they have the morals of a cat.

Is the case going to slow to suit them? The client will remind you that other attorneys might be interested in the case. Have you reached a settlement on a contingency fee case which has less dollars than the client wanted? Well, you don't really need to collect your entire, fee, don't you? After all, the client is the one who suffered the pain, as the client will remind you.

When the client writes a letter to the other attorney admitting damaging things (without consulting you first, of course), they'll defiantly tell you that it's your fault--they wanted to cut through the legal stuff with a direct approach.

As an attorney, on the other hand, your duty is to give your client dog-like loyalty through good times and bad. A client can fire you for no reason and at any time with a wave of the hand. An attorney has to make a motion, serve the client by certified mail, and convince a frowning judge that he or she can no longer represent the client. Even then, the judge can force you to represent the client--even if you're owed thousands in fees.

And it is truly heartwarming to see how quickly a client will turn on you if he or she will benefit from it. It doesn't matter that you called in favors and twisted arms to get that client a sweet deal on that felony; if she thinks she can get a slightly better deal after the plea goes down, she won't turn a hair in alleging incompetence to try to overturn the plea.

Heaven forbid that the case should run into serious trouble. The client will disappear under the bed quicker than a cat in an earthquake. The lawyer (who usually promised the court that the client could be trusted out of custody, no matter the new charges) stands stammering in front of a raging judge, trying to dodge a contempt charge.

Inevitably, your client will fail to obey a direct order of the court. Can they take responsibility for themselves? Not on a bet. Every attorney who's ever stood with a client in court has heard the refrain: My lawyer told me I didn't have to. My lawyer didn't explain things to me. My lawyer said she'd take care of it.

And, after all this, if by some twist of ramshackle fate you should win the case, the client will tell you that there was no way you could lose, ask you to cut your fee, and wonder aloud if another attorney couldn't have gotten an acquittal *and* an apology.

Expect it all, my dear friend. If you're lucky, you might hear "thanks." More often, you'll end up in a dispute over fees. Do not expect gratitude from a client. You might as well try to teach a cat to fetch.

FORTY THINGS I'VE LEARNED SINCE I WAS THIRTY

1. If you want to keep it clean, don't give it to a two-year-old.

2. If someone is shouting at you, one of you isn't listening.

3. People who tell you how to live your life are usually giving themselves advice. But they don't take themselves seriously enough to follow it.

4. Something good sells itself.

5. Good friends are hard to find and harder to lose, thank God.

6. Life is a mystery until you have a child. Then, it's just very busy.

7. Sooner or later, everything you get paid regularly for doing becomes a job, even fun things.

8. No one wants to lie, but no one can avoid it.

9. Large pleasures surprise us; small pleasures keep us sane.

10. Don't be afraid to change your dreams.

11. Once you discover how to do the thing you really love, the rest of your life makes more sense.

12. Life is made up of long periods of boredom interrupted by short bursts of terror.

13. Focus, but don't obsess.

14. Familiarity breeds children.

15. Children, lovers and the IRS get mad when you ignore them.

16. You are the worst judge of your own work; either you're too stern or you're too forgiving.

17. Avoid people who want to be punished.

18. Job, Jewish, argued with God and was rewarded. Paul, a Christian, obeyed God and was martyred. Yet we wonder why there are so many Jewish lawyers and Christian soldiers.

19. A day off is not a day wasted.

20. If you're still accomplishing things, you're not depressed.

21. Unless it's a disaster, it's an irritation.

22. Vent. Then forget it.

23. An artist is not responsible to society, to family, not even to themselves; an artist is only responsible to the truth.

24. Be careful, not timid.

25. Don't let a misunderstanding fester.

26. Crazy friends are fun up to the minute that they almost get you killed.

27. Crazy lovers are fun up to the minute that they start calling you at 3 a.m. to make sure you're not sleeping with somebody else.

28. As soon as someone is put in charge of other people, they change.

29. Even the most benevolent bureaucracy involves politics.

30. Once you bail someone out of jail, your relationship changes.

31. You don't look down the barrel of a gun and pull the trigger to see if it's loaded; you don't flirt with a single woman by talking about getting married.

32. If you're not sure you should say something, you shouldn't.

33. God is smarter than we think He is.

34. At the end of a court case, the only person who is satisfied is the lawyer who won.

35. Pay extra now for the person who knows how to do it and is licensed, or pay more later for that same person to fix what the unlicensed person screwed up.

36. Things can be replaced. People can only be missed.

37. You end up focusing on the things that are important to you, even if you don't realize they're important to you.

38. Aim to be content. Hope to be surprised by happiness.

39. All judges think they're doing the right thing, even when you show them that they're not.

40. As Epictetus, the Greek Stoic Philosopher said, you can control only three things: Your thoughts, your actions, your responses. All else is beyond your control. So lighten up on yourself and everyone else. There is a reason why my blood pressure is healthy despite the job I do and the life I lead.

Future Jeopardy

"Make sure the client gets a copy of that letter," he said. The Secretary beeped to indicate it had registered the request. He put down the audio mouse for a second and realized for one brief nostalgic moment that he actually missed the old days when there was a human being on the other end of the steno pad. You could hardly compliment a computer about how it was dressed today, or talk to it about the latest episode of *L.A. Law, The Next Generation.* Certainly, a computer was cheaper, quicker, and more efficient; but he somehow missed the human contact.

The Secretary beeped for him, and the electronic voice (he had chosen the female voice, aged 25) said "Department 82 on Virtual Reality line 4 is ready to hear your motion. Shall I ask them for second call, sir?" (The last honorific he had asked to be programmed in. In fact, none of his human secretaries had *ever* called him "sir.")

"No, I'll go ahead and argue now." He donned the goggles and plugged into the port for Superior Court Virtual Reality. Suddenly, he was standing in the spic and span courtroom of Department 82, dressed in a blue pin-striped suit. He was actually dressed in a sweatshirt and jeans, but you could have the computer dress you any way you wanted in the VR port.

The judge sat at her bench, a blue tie peeking out through her black robe. She looked like her hair had just been coiffed at an expensive salon, but he knew that it was only a computer-generated hairdo. In truth, she was probably in curlers and blue jeans. In fact, he was sure that Dept. 82 itself was probably a run-down, paper-strewn rat trap of a room. That's why he hated going to trial--it ruined his mental image of the VR courtrooms.

27

"Mr. Watson, are you ready to argue your motion?" The judge asked.

"Certainly your honor."

"And Ms. Smith--Ms. Smith, you`d better adjust your image."

He looked over and saw a tentacled monster wearing a bright baby-blue jumpsuit. These big firm lawyers always pulled this stunt--try to rattle the opposition by looking like an alien before the motion. The image wobbled, and a woman with steel gray hair suddenly popped into the jumpsuit. He almost asked for sanctions for her use of the old trick, but the judge cut him off.

"That had better not happen again, Ms. Smith. If I find you in contempt, you'll be sharing a cell with the Mario Brothers. Mr. Watson, you said you`d have a reply for us today regarding the opposition to your motion. Why haven't we received it?"

"We sent it through yesterday, but all the lines were down due to the court's little problem."

The judge sighed. "We certainly had some difficulties when that one bug popped up. Turned all of our computer-filed pleadings into `Jabborwocky.' Though. the way some lawyers write, it was hard to notice the difference at first. I suspect the bug was the work of that anti-lawyer group, the Quayle League. We`ll catch them someday, and then I'll put them into a reality they`re going to regret. Do you have the reply now?"

The Secretary had already sent the pleading to the court before she asked. There was a moment of silence, as the court's LawClerk program checked the cites and rendered an opinion. The judge grunted.

"Looks like your case is better than Ms. Smith's case. Is there any argument?"

Ms. Smith did, indeed, put up an argument, but the judge didn't seem impressed. The image was that of an impassive jurist, but Watson was sure that the judge was actually reading the newspaper while Ms. Smith droned on. It was hard to argue against the court`s LawClerk computer.

"The motion is granted," the judge finally said. "Are we ever going to trial on this?"

"I would like to set a Status Conference as soon as possible," Watson said. Ms. Smith was silent.

"You'll be number 1,247 on the Monday calendar. You may have to have a pseudo-Commissioner set dates and time limits." That meant another computer-generated personality. Well, Watson thought, at least they were predictable.

"That's fine with me," Watson said. Ms. Smith nodded in assent. The Secretary printed out a minute order, complete with proof of service as the image of Department 82 flickered. Ms. Smith turned to Watson before fading out.

"See you in court," she said, turning into the alien for a brief second.

"Not if I see you first," Watson muttered as he took the goggles off.

BLAMING THE QUAKE

One of the more encouraging signs of recovery around Southern California in the weeks after the Northridge Quake was the way that all of us seemed to come together as a community and implicitly agree to use the earthquake as an excuse for every conceivable problem.

Clients were the first to catch on, of course. Not a single attorney between Ventura and the Orange County line was paid a dime in fees in January because the quake seemed to magically wipe out every client's bank account.

Others in the legal community were eager to sign on. Secretaries did nothing to earn their wages--but suddenly had a legitimate excuse for filing their nails instead of filing pleadings. Paralegals couldn't meet deadlines--a piece of news which has the equivalent shock value of dog-bites-man--and were able to blame the Quake. Even court clerks, who usually wouldn't apologize to St. Peter for losing the keys to the Pearly Gates, were able to justifiably tell lawyers and litigants that their cases had literally fallen through the cracks.

Since most lawyers tend to make their living by making excuses for their clients, the Quake soon became a growth industry in the courthouses. For procrastinating lawyers, the quake was a godsend. I wouldn't be surprised to discover that it was engineered by some big downtown firm to avoid an OSC on sanctions in Van Nuys Superior.

The Quake Excuses used by lawyers seemed to fall most often into two categories:

THE QUAKE ATE MY HOMEWORK.
This was used to explain why something wasn't done on

time:

"I realize we were supposed to respond to your discovery request to produce documents which would be devastating to our case, but after the quake, who can find any papers?"

"Of course I was ready to respond to the motion today, your honor, and I know opposing counsel has cited a case which seems dead on point and which will legally string my client up by his toes, but I can guarantee the court I had a very persuasive case which refuted my opponents--I just can't find my research notes after the quake."

"We were perfectly ready to go to trial today, your honor, but our witnesses (which we had managed to track down on January 16, after diligent investigation, but too late to be divulged in discovery) have now all vanished because, wouldn't you know it, *every one of them* lived in an apartment which has been red-tagged. Could we get a three month continuance? "

THE QUAKE MADE ME DO IT.

These excuses were used to explain inexplicable behavior:

"I realize my client has bench warranted for the sixth time, your honor, but he's afraid to come into the courthouse after the quake. Could we get a change of venue?"

"My client took the stereo from that red-tagged apartment by mistake, your honor. With the valley having moved over a whole inch, he went into the wrong door without looking."

"Yes, it's true my client took off for Barbados this morning with a suitcase stuffed with $1 Million of corporation funds, but he's just going to preserve corporate assets from further damage until the aftershocks stop."

Like all good things, however, the Quake Excuses will not last forever. There's going to be a statute of limitations in the minds of judges on using the Quake to excuse not filing motions. I, for one, do not want to be in the courtroom when some hapless lawyer tries to convince a Federal Judge in

May that he didn't respond to a motion because his office is still disrupted from the earthquake. The explosion from the bench will make that poor soul *wish* the earth had swallowed him on January17.

Right Idea, Wrong Mission:

A Reply to Hon. Clay M. Smith

Recently, I almost destroyed my television set.

It happened during Monday Night Football. A commercial came on for a show called *The Practice*.

The allegedly handsome defense attorney was looking into the mirror, washing his face. He said to the mirror (and, by extension to us, the viewers) "People ask me how I can go to court and defend people accused of the lowest, most despicable crimes, the scum of the earth."

I was ready to hear some ringing declaration about the rights of the accused, the time-honored role of the lawyer, or even something about it actually being fun. Instead this "lawyer" looked at the camera with puppy eyes and said, "Don't ask."

I nearly tossed an iron through the tube. This is the guy that ABC was putting forward as the lawyer you want in your corner when the chips are down?

As a defense attorney, I am often asked the same question. I prefer to answer, as did Orange County Assistant Public Defender Debbie Kwast, when asked how she could defend "criminals":

"I don't defend criminals," she said, "I defend people."

This little incident came back to me when I was reading, with growing astonishment, the recent article by the Hon. Clay M. Smith in the December issue of *Orange County Lawyer*. In the article, the Hon. Judge Smith suggested that the criminal justice system--judiciary, prosecution, defense bar--get together and write a mission statement.

This is not a bad idea. Far too often I have found that people involved in bringing "justice" to the community forget what we're there for. Trials, plea bargains, and other proceedings become personal matters, and we lose our perspective. A mission statement which truly encompasses the hundreds of years judicial and lawyerly wisdom could be a touchstone for those who practice law with good intent.

But when I read what the good judge proposed was the *purpose* of the criminal justice system, I fell out of my chair. I was incredulous that a jurist of the regard and experience of Judge Smith could suggest that we are here to "redress crime and punish the guilty."

In other words, we're here to get convictions. We're here for revenge. We're here to make sure that criminals do not go free. Foolish me, I had always thought that punishment was the province of the jails and prisons.

The good judge has made the same mistake as the actor playing the lawyer on "The Practice." He assumes that everyone accused of a crime is guilty. He goes even further--he assumes that a crime has been committed in the first place.

I suppose it is to be expected. Increasingly, our society has adopted a perception that the ancient and venerable rights of a speedy trial, and a fair and just trial, are too burdensome and oppressive for today's world. Innocent until proven guilty? That's too hard on our prosecutors. They should be able to convict people easier than that. Beyond a reasonable doubt? Too tough on our hard working criminal justice system. A guilty man might go free. Better that we take the chance of convicting the innocent than that we release someone accused of a crime for which he might be guilty.

The flaw, of course, is that we have seen other systems fail which have adopted the "guilty until proven innocent" standard. Innocent men and women were imprisoned and executed. When their innocence was finally demonstrated, there was no redress.

Under such a system, no one is safe. All it takes is an accusation about a heinous crime and a person can lose everything, no matter whether the evidence is there or not.

Also, our society's present perception that criminals are getting away with everything from trespassing to murder is just plain wrong. At least 95% of the criminal cases filed in California end up in conviction. A vast majority of those cases result in jail or prison time.

Yet I have to agree with one thing: There should be a mission statement in our system. However, it should be a statement that truly reflects the purpose of the system, and the roles each of us play in that system.

So let me suggest an alternative mission statement:

The criminal justice system exists to hold evidentiary hearings, usually trials, to determine whether a crime has been committed and whether the person accused was the one who committed the crime. The freedom of a person in our society is so precious that we will accept nothing less than proof beyond a reasonable doubt on both of those points before we will brand a person a criminal and make him or her subject to criminal penalty.

As participants in this system, we all agree to act with the utmost ethics so that anyone accused of a crime receives a timely, full and fair hearing. This means that if a prosecutor or a judge realizes that there is no evidence to support a conviction, the case will be dismissed. This means that the defense attorneys will litigate vigorously but ethically on behalf of their clients, for only when such advocacy has been expended in the service of an accused can we be sure that the hearing has been full and fair.

And we will make no snap judgments about someone just because they are accused of a crime. After all, those on trial are not criminals; they're people.

The RICH LAWYER

The client was trying to get me to cut my bill. I had won her case for her, had retrieved for her a sizeable amount of money that had been frozen in escrow, had sent her enemies scattering in terror across the legal field of battle.

Together we scanned the horizon, the broken bodies of the defendant's legal arguments littering the field. She called me, after I mailed her the bill, and said, in that time-honored greeting of a client when the day has been won:

"This is too much money to pay. I need you to cut the bill."

It is proverbial, the gratitude of kings and clients. One might as well look for gratitude in a cat.

To top it all off, though, she twisted the knife a little deeper and said, "What are you worried about? You're an attorney. You have lots of money."

Ah, there it is. I'm an attorney, therefore I have lots of money. I belong in the same class as Melvin Belli, Richard Nixon and F. Lee Bailey. I drive a Mercedes, eat at expensive restaurants, and date movie stars.

My client actually believes this, even though she's been to my humble office (a small house which the owner converted to law suites; I call it "The Little Law Office on the Prairie.") She's seen me turn to my humble Panasonic word processor (not computer, mind you) and type out a declaration we needed immediately because I have only 10 hours of secretarial help available to me each week. She's seen me drive up to court in my humble volkswagen, with more mileage on it than a WWII jeep--and just as battered. She's even noticed, I'll bet, that my briefcase is frayed on the edges and has a torn zipper at the top.

Yet I'm a rich attorney. So I can take a hit on her bill. She, after all, is merely a property owner with thousands in liquid assets, and she has to watch each penny carefully.

I am tempted to ask her how she thinks lawyers become rich. I can guarantee you, it is not part of the job description. Long hours and intense aggravation, yes; riches, not necessarily.

In the end I reluctantly agree to a reduction in the bill. After all, we have to maintain good relations with clients because half of our referrals come from previous customers.

I wonder, though, as I accept the check for hundreds of dollars less, what she would have done long ago if one of her employers had told her, "You did a good job, but I'm going to pay you less than you earned because you already have money in the bank."

I know, I know. She would have called a lawyer. Probably a rich one.

Trial Animals

There's an old game we played—actually, were forced to play—in school as a child: If you could be any kind of animal, what would you be?

Me, I always tried to find the animals that would make the teachers scratch their heads. "An armadillo?" one would ask, with that tone in their voice that showed they, native Californians, were barely aware of what an armadillo was, had never seen one lying martyred by the side of a stretch of road outside of El Paso.

I because I have seen all sorts of fauna in our trial courtrooms, and have scientifically classified the more prevalent beasts for your education. Look over the list below. Which type of trial animal are you?

The Lion is what we all once aspired to become. This king or queen of trial beasts knows when to roar, when to hunt prey and when to sleep in the shade on a particularly hot day. In the courtroom, this person regally walks in, is perfectly dressed, has a loud booming voice when stirred, and can smell a witness' fear. In fact, a witness' fear rouses the beast to become more ruthless in questioning.

The Hyena likes to believe he or she is one of the more regal beasts of the trial courts, but, in fact, the only thing they share in common with the Lion is that they tend to be very loud. Typically, the Hyena is a scavenger, picking up the scraps of cases other animals leave behind, which usually puts them in a poor position during trial. They make up for this by being totally inaccurate in their understanding of the law—and they compensate for this by being inaccurate in a very loud manner.

The Monkey is a very clever trial beast, one who can slip case cites and statutes into arguments from memory,

38

usually with volume and page numbers. The Monkey talks incessantly, usually very quickly, and about a tenth of what the Monkey says is actually relevant. You have to discover which tenth.

The Elephant tends to move very slowly at trial, and cannot be rushed by anything—not even the Lion. The Elephant knows the law inside and out—so long as you're talking about the law ten years ago. The Elephant rarely reads new cases because he or she really, really likes the old ones. When the Elephant crosses a witness, he or she tends to meander around the subject as if they've got all year. Beware: In an Elephant's slow mind, they *do* have all year.

The Snake usually tries to pull a number of questionable stunts on his or her opponent during trial, some of which work. Unctuous to a fault to the judge, the snake can turn around and swallow your case whole, then assume an expression of innocence on his or her face, even as the large lump that was your client is working its way down the scaly belly of the beast.

The Gorilla just wants to be left alone to scratch himself and eat bananas. This beast rarely goes to trial, as he believes that beating on his chest and making loud noises is usually enough to scare off a trial and make the parties settle. But the Gorilla, if roused, can be a powerful adversary, crushing you in his hairy paw just to get rid of you. It's nothing personal, really. You should've let him sleep.

The Gazelle is beautiful to look at, usually very well dressed and very well spoken. The Gazelle will tell you how much they love trial work and how wonderful their case is. But when it comes time to settle or go to trial, the Gazelle's powerful survival instinct will cause it to disappear like yesterday's news. If forced to go to trial, the Gazelle will continually look like there's a lion two feet behind, and will attempt to finish the trial as quickly as he or she can. They don't care if they win or lose—they just want out of the veldt at feeding time.

The Shrike is a peculiar creature, one that usually will accuse its opponent of unethical and slimy tactics, no matter what the opponent actually does. The Shrike makes a lot of noise about his or her client's rights but, strangely enough, very little about the actual case or its merits.

What trial type are you? If you recognized yourself here, what can you do to improve yourself and become a lion? Or do you even want to be a lion? Is there another beast I haven't talked about—and there are hundreds more I could discuss—that you believe represents your nature at trial?

I, for one, tend to be more of a hound than a lion in trial—I am loyal to the client, I am quick witted on the hunt (I like to believe so, at least) and I trust my instincts. But I'm not that great a dresser and I certainly don't have the royal mien that accompanies the lion's entrance.

But I feel comfortable in my dogginess. How about you? If you were a trial animal, what type of trial animal would you be?

The Zen of Control

In my youth there was a television show called *Kung Fu.* It was about a man with an American father and a Chinese mother who trains in a Buddhist monastery to become a monk, but has to flee to America. The show was famous for its flashbacks where a blind monk would teach the young boy Zen lessons, then would whup his little yellow robed behind in sparring, just to reinforce the lesson. The old guy called the hero "grasshopper" with such comments as, "Ah, Grasshopper, you must first know yourself before you can know the Way."

I think about Grasshopper and the monk when I see lawyers trying to "control" the courtroom, and merely being rude and alienating everyone. I know that such lawyers have taken trial seminars in which they have been told that they have to pull bush league stunts to rattle the opposition into submission.

For instance, some seminars teach that you have to be the one who speaks first in court, the one who controls the conversation by not letting the other side get a word in edgewise. This jack-in-the-box tactic has the unpleasant side effect of having counsel popping up from their tables at odd moments, rudely shouting or talking when someone else is trying to make a point. While such a tactic might work for radio talk show hosts—who can, after all, hang up on their callers—in court it's likely to result in sanctions.

Some seminars say that you should, early on, spread out your materials to take up space on the opposition's side as well as yours. This is the territorial imperative theory: The more space you occupy, the more important you are. But my problem with this is that I will *never* let someone

41

occupy space on a table set aside for me. I have my own materials to spread out so that they are handy. If you try to intrude, I will push your stuff back toward you. If you do it again, I'll put it on the floor. If you do it a third time, I'll point out to the judge that you're trying to control his courtroom by taking up too much space, and I'll ask for sanctions.

Chances are, the lawyers who don't put up a fight when you dip into their space aren't noticing very much to begin with. So your brilliant tactic is lost on the dull.

Another little tactic which sometimes backfires is to object as much as you can, even when the objection is not well taken. The idea here is that you will rattle the opposing attorney, throw him or her off of rhythm, make him or her sweat for every bit of evidence they get. By the time direct examination is done, the story is so disjointed and incomplete that the jury isn't sure what's happened.

Most experienced trial lawyers know the great danger of this tactic. Unless your objections are valid, and unless the judge actually sustains a few of them, objecting for objection's sake merely marks you as a tricky lawyer, one who is so afraid of the evidence against your client that you will do anything to stonewall. The judge, as well, will be so exasperated with you by the end of direct examination that his or her demeanor toward you will inevitably be hostile. Even the fairest of judges is only human.

By the time you're finished with your objections, everyone in the courtroom will hate you: The judge, the jury, the opposition, the bailiff, the clerk, the court reporter—especially the court reporter. All you will end up controlling is your temper when you lose the case.

Yet we've all seen that golden trial lawyer who can walk into a courtroom and make a statement by his or her very presence. We've all been spellbound by their elegance of thought, their sharp questions, their ability to control the proceedings from beginning to end with instinctual ease. How do these lawyers control the courtroom? Because, make no mistake, they are in control, much to your client's detriment.

As far as I can see, it really comes down to old fashioned preparation. The lawyer who controls the case usually knows the case inside and out. He or she has the facts and the witnesses at fingertips' reach. A detailed trial notebook usually accompanies them into court. They know the law of the case, the recent decisions, the statutes. Their command of procedure is impeccable.

The lawyer who controls the case knows how to ask direct, effective questions of his or her witnesses, and has already thought out ahead of time how to ask such questions so that they are not subject to objection. He or she has already planned the cross examination of every witness in the same manner.

Such a lawyer speaks with confidence because he or she *is* confident. They know so much about what's going on in the case that they're talking to the judge at a much different level than the opposition. Watching such a lawyer try a case against a barely prepared litigator is like watching that Kung Fu character tell some threatening outlaw "I mean no harm." You just know the next thing that will happen is that the outlaw will be flying unconscious through the air and Grasshopper will be standing there like nothing happened.

It's just as the Zen masters would say, were they to train litigators: To control the courtroom, you first must control yourself, Grasshopper.

A Bit of Heresy

All good trial lawyers can tell you the anecdote of the defense lawyer in a mayhem trial, in which his client was accused of biting another man's earlobe off. An eyewitness was testifying, and stated on direct that he didn't actually see the defendant bite the earlobe off. The defense attorney, spotting the flaw, rose imperiously and glared at the eyewitness.

"How, sir, can you say that it was my client who bit this man's earlobe if you didn't see it happen?"

"Because," the witness meekly explained, "I saw him spit it out."

This cautionary tale is used to accompany a bit of doctrine in the litigation universe: Never ask a question on cross examination to which you do not already know the answer. Usually, it's a pretty good rule. But, like all rules, a good lawyer knows at least three exceptions to it.

The most prevalent scenerio is the "nothing to lose" paradigm. (I love using those big words. It makes me feel so legal.) In this setting, you are embroiled in a case for which there seems to be no escape. The evidence against your client is extremely damaging, and the judge has been idly drawing little nooses in his trial notes. You're really worried about this, because this is a misdemeanor case.

Then a witness against your client will say something intriguing. "I'm pretty sure it was Mr. Smith who was running from the store when the alarm went off." You scan your police report quickly. In the report it only says that the witness was "positive" that it was your client. You can either exploit the difference between "positive" or "pretty sure"—the safe thing to do, given what you know—or you

44

can go into uncharted territory hoping for a bit of luck.

"What do you mean by 'pretty sure'? Is there something that might have affected your ability to see the man who was running out of the store?"

Now, this is heresy. You might get a "spit it out" type of answer—eg, the witness might say, "Well, I saw him with the stolen merchandise a few seconds later, so I thought back and realized it was Smith I saw running out of the store." In which case, your bad case is still bad. But remember, the scenerio is that you have nothing to lose. At this point in the trial it's just one more brick in the wall.

On the other hand, the witness might give you some daylight. "Well, he wasn't wearing the same shirt I saw him wearing two minutes later." Or, "I just glanced at the guy running out of the door before I stepped back to avoid getting hit by a bus. Later, when the police showed me your client, he looked a lot like the guy I saw for a second." This, at least, gives you something to argue. Obviously, though, the attorney has to be able to assess the state of his or her case when the chance is taken.

The second time you might ask a question whose answer is not known is when a witness surprises you on the stand by saying something damaging about himself, or about the complaining witness. Even if you have no prior evidence on this, you should explore it on cross.

"Mr. Jones, you say that you've only been arrested one time. What was that for?" Any relevance objection is swatted away by noting that the witness put the issue into play by bringing it up on direct.

If you're lucky, the witness will admit that he's been convicted of perjury in the past. But even if it's merely an assault and battery on an inanimate object, the witness has now gone down a peg from upstanding citizen to someone who's been *arrested*. No amount of explaining will get that bad taste out of the jury's mouth. There is no bad response to your question.

Third, sometimes the legal fates will smile upon you and deliver the witness into your hands. There will be a question on an unknown subject whose answer cannot possibly hurt you

I once had a client who was charged with trying to cash in his father's savings account. The client was somewhat loopy, and kept insisting that his evil twin, a man named Tom, had actually tried to commit the crime. It had been a family joke for years, the client said, that he and Tom were twins, even though they were only cousins. Our investigation could not find the evil twin. I was sure the client had watched too many episodes of *The Patty Duke Show*. The bank had pictures of my very peculiar-looking client attempting the crime.

At trial the father testified that he did not give his son permission to cash in the account. Since my client was not going to testify, I asked the father the question to which there was, truly, no bad answer:

"Is there a man named Tom, a family friend, who looks like your son?"

I figured that if the father said no, the jury would have no idea of what I was talking about and disregard it. And it would make the client happy that I'd asked it, because it showed that I was paying attention to him.

As luck would have it, the father's face suddenly fell.

"Yes," he said, "Tom *does* look like my son."

I felt as if I'd been struck by lightning. I then asked a series of questions to flesh out the existence of the evil twin. Suddenly, a hopeless case had hope.

Had I adhered to the orthodoxy, I would never have asked the question because I didn't know what the father would say. Instead, a selective use of heresy put the case in doubt. And, after all, doubt is what we look for in the defense, *verdad?*

Working Backwards

In E.B. White's book *The Once and Future King,* Merlin the Magician is so wise because he's been living his life backwards. Instead of growing into an old man, he is growing into a young man. Instead of experiencing time continuously forward, he's been seeing it backwards, so he could know our future because it was actually his past.

Merlin is actually a pretty good model if you're preparing for trial. The best preparation is to work backwards from the final argument to discovery.

The typical trial lawyer prepares a case from the complaint to the trial. He or she looks over the charging document or civil complaint, separates out the elements which have to be proved, and begins working on those elements. Not a bad way to do it, but there's always something you've missed. When the time comes to commence trial, and you're working on your opening statement, there are inevitably gaps of facts you wish you'd had the foresight to ferret out.

But if you work backwards from the final argument, you stumble across those needed facts. The final argument, after all, is the culmination of the trial. It's where you tie the facts and the law together to show the finder of fact why your client must win. And, let's face it, it's the part of the trial that's the most fun.

One day as I was preparing for a complex civil case (back in my days at the big LA law firm) I was rather bored with the interrogatories and depositions. We were still in the middle of discovery, and I was only the second chair, so it was unlikely I'd ever get even a moment in the spotlight at trial. Nonetheless, on my way home that night, I playacted the final argument I would give in the case.

47

"Our client is a widow, whose husband was lost in a traffic accident one rainy night. He left them with a business and an insurance policy and little else."

Wait a minute, I thought, is that right? What else did our client leave his wife with? Were there other assets which might come into play?

"Her child is autistic, and difficult to raise. But the plaintiff says that during the funeral, in full view of everyone assembled, she promised to pay 'back' a 'debt' of $100,000 the late husband supposedly owed to the brother."

Wait a minute, I thought again, who heard this promise? Did we ask that, or did we assume that since it was the brother's family and the wife was considered an outsider that no one would deny the story. Anyway, we need to know from the plaintiff who they say heard this statement, so that we can take their depositions. That hadn't been done yet.

"The brother says that he was owed $100,000 from a loan he had made a year before, a loan the wife knew nothing about."

How did the brother get this kind of money? He wasn't wealthy, nor was the family. The husband had worked his way up from nothing to buy a business and an insurance policy. More discovery danced in my head.

By the end of my fantasy argument, I had three pages of notes on facts we had to determine, either through discovery or investigation. By the end of the case I knew more about the evil brother's case than he did. Working backwards I had been able to spot things which working only with the complaint I would never have divined.

In going over the final argument, I also ran into gaps in the law that had to be researched. Is an oral promise to repay valid? Can a wife promise to repay money from an insurance policy to which she was only a partial beneficiary? If there is no writing, can money given to a family member be considered a loan or a gift?

Hidden legal issues suddenly blossomed before my eyes. I also started looking at the jury instructions for the case, even though jury instructions are usually one of the last things a lawyer gathers. I realized there were some gaps in the BAJI that we had to make up by specials.

And, in going over the final argument, the best and worst way to approach a case occurred to me. We had been going on the angle of a poor widowed woman with an autistic child, and the hardship it would bring on them. The client, of course, had adamantly denied ever promising to pay any money to the evil brother. In going over the final argument, I realized that the poor widow angle would not work—it was too patronizing to the client. Instead, we re-tooled our strategy to call into question the existence of the debt, the alleged promise, and the legality of such a promise even had it been made.

I learned that going over the final argument gives the trial lawyer a chance to see the facts vital to the case; the law which may not be apparent in the complaint and answer; the tactics which would play best to a jury or judge. It also gave the case a framework for organizing evidence and law. And it made me enthusiastic about the case—I found that knowing so much about a trial made me eager to go to work in the morning.

In the end we were able to knock out the case through summary judgment. The widow and autistic child kept their money, the brother slunk off into the darkness and the trial disappeared. And that's magic even Merlin would have been proud of.

Do Not Feed the Clerks

Young lawyer, if you wish to make a name for yourself in the trial courts of this land, there is someone you must respect above all others: The clerk of the courtroom.

Oh, the judge may love you and the bailiff may laugh at your jokes (if you can get him to look up from his *Guns and Ammo* magazine, that is), but you will get nowhere in the legal system if the clerks think you are an arrogant twit.

You may think that clerks merely push papers around, write down what the judge tells them, and play video solitaire on the courtroom computer. And, while much of that is true, it is also deceptive and dangerous to think of the clerks as, well, merely clerks.

As a test, take two similar courtrooms. Try to get two judges as similar as possible, and bring in two cases as similar as possible.

In the first courtroom, treat the clerk like a clod of dirt. Be arrogant, angry, contemptuous. When a clerk tries to tell you how something is done in her courtroom, wave her off and sniff, "I don't see *your* license to practice law on the wall. Unless it's being hidden by those pictures of zoo monkeys...your kids? Hard to tell." It also helps to throw in a comment about how inefficient and worm-brained most government workers are, and about how much smarter you are because, after all, you finished college.

You will notice that your cases always seem to be heard last. The file disappears with alarming regularity. Status conferences are scheduled without your knowledge and you end up missing a lot of them, resulting in hundreds of dollars in sanctions imposed. You swear to the judge that nothing was calendared, but this just seems to make him more angry.

Worse, you will see the judge snarl and sneer at you every time you appear in front of him. He will call into question you judgment and legal acumen. Your motions will be routinely denied with sarcastic comments.

And heaven help you if you go to trial in that courtroom. By the time the jury gets the verdict forms, they'll be ready to send *you* to jail--even if it's a civil case. And you'll know who to blame, too. The jury may not, by law, be allowed to take a cue from the judge as to which way to vote, but the jury instruction says nothing about the clerks.

In the second courtroom, treat the clerks with respect and an admiration bordering on awe. Say things like, "Did you have to give up your modeling career to become a clerk?" Or tell them, "You must be a genius to keep track of all this paperwork." Never demand anything. If you need priority, ask for it apologetically. Tell them that any fool could be a lawyer--just like the guy opposite you in this case (nudge), but it takes someone with saintly patience and herculean strength to be a clerk. Tell them that you hope your kids grow up to become clerks.

Remember to tell them, in a non-threatening and pleasant way, that the outfit they're wearing today makes them look very attractive. Ask if they've lost weight. Ask if that's a new hairdo or if they've recently been to a health spa. And don't forget the occasional infusion of chocolate into their courtroom candy jars--a legal substance which has the delightful quality of calming even the most frazzled clerk.

In this courtroom you will notice that you can work miracles. Your motions will pull rabbits out of their legal hats, no matter what the law. Your faults will be overlooked or cherished. You will be in on every courtroom joke. You can ask them to find a file dating from before California was admitted to the state, and the dusty old thing will appear on counsel table shortly after lunch. And if you ask for priority, you'll be out of the courtroom so quick that you won't have to pay a penny in

51

parking fees.

If you are fortunate to go to trial in this courtroom, it will pass like a week in Hawaii. The judge will treat you like a relative. The bailiff will wink at you and offer to lend you his copy of *Guns and Ammo.* The jury will want to take you home for dinner.

Your clients will believe that you are the greatest lawyer in the country. The opposing lawyers will ask for your card. Every unmarried person in the courtroom will want you to help them produce children.

All for treating the clerks like something a little better than human. After all, it's nothing less than they deserve for putting up with dozens of lawyers every day.

So, young lawyer, take note. Remember where the power in any bureaucracy lies: In the paperwork. Take care of the clerks, and the clerks will take care of you.

And for those court clerks who happen to be reading this, please remember that I, of all people, know that your professionalism would *never* allow your distaste of an arrogant attorney to interfere with your sworn duties. I know that you do your job ethically and competently and to the best of your ability--and, my, aren't you looking particularly attractive in that outfit today?

The Club

A young attorney once sat in my humble office, in my solo days, encased in a $500 suit and fiddling with his cell phone. He'd come to talk to me about a civil case in which we opposed one another. After some initial pleasantries such as the traditional comparison of law schools, and some general agreement as to how tough the law business was, he came to his point:

"I wanted to come here personally to talk to you about resolving the case."

"I'm always ready to talk," I said.

"I know I could convince my client to swallow his costs if the case was dismissed."

"How terribly generous," I snapped, disappointed that he wasn't offering even a smattering of settlement. "But you know that won't work. We are willing to talk numbers, however."

He looked uncomfortable at that and put the cell phone into his pocket.

"I can't do that. The client won't pay a dime to settle."

"Well, I guess we won't settle," I said. Then he made an unforgettable, fantastical, chimerical statement:

"I thought you'd agree to dismiss as a favor to me. After all, we're both lawyers, we're in the same club."

I was astounded. He hurried out of my office, no doubt terrified by the Greek mask of comedy my expression suddenly resembled.

In the same club? So I was to abandon my client's interests and cave in to him just because we're both children of the Great God Lex? My lord, I felt like asking him, what do you think a lawyer is *supposed* to do?

As the years have passed, I think of that deluded young

man from time to time. I especially recall the statement when a case stops being about the clients' problems and starts to become a vendetta between the lawyers. When all is said and done, the lawyers slink back to their lairs and the clients are left to stare at each other, wondering what in the hell just happened.

Prosecutors see this all the time. Some ex-DA will trundle into the courtroom and try to insinuate himself into the graces of the calendar deputy by recalling his own days as a prosecutor in Podunk County. Then he'll inevitably use the line, "When I was a DA, we never would have even filed a case like this."

Why this insult is supposed to charm a prosecutor-- particularly a harried prosecutor in a busy court--is a process of thought I can't comprehend. I think it goes back to my young adversary all those years ago: We're all in the same club, so give me this one this time.

I suppose, in a way, we *are* in the same club. We have overcome similar obstacles, share similar schooling; all of us have learned to "think like a lawyer," and we have the same arguments with our spouses or significant others. And I'm sure we all scream objections at the TV screen when watching dumb lawyer shows.

But why should this somehow magically transform us all into bosom buddies who will sell out our clients for the sake of an old clubmate? Aren't we also trained to understand that the lawyer on the other side of the table would capture and eat our client, if it would help his case?

Sorry friends. I will do favors for people in this world, and I will trust that the people I do such favors for will remember them when I need a blessing from them. The problem is, none of those people happen to belong to the club.

Controlling Behavior

On a particularly bizarre episode of *LA Law*, an entertainment lawyer, who had always wanted to be a dancer, decided that he would impress his movie mogul client. He tap-danced through the court proceedings. He'd stutter step up to the witness, pirouette to pick up a document, and spin into a grand finale during final argument.

Later, he explained that he was only trying to "gain control of the courtroom," as he had heard over and over in the trial practice seminars. His way was to call such attention to himself that everything else was overshadowed.

Most of the judges I know would have had the man in ankle irons before the day was out. (A few would have joined him in the grand finale.) But the poor lawyer's dilemma remains a serious one for all beginning litigators: How do you assert your presence in the courtroom without looking particularly arrogant?

First, let me commit a piece of heresy here. We are always told by the experts to gain control of the courtroom, as if we were merely dogs fighting over a bone. I have seen a number of lawyers try to pull such silly tricks as putting extra books and files on part of the opposition's table, always trying to speak first, popping up like a jack in the box to be sure they were the ones who reached sidebar first, and trying to out yell the opposition.

These are merely tricks, and the jury sees them as such. You will hear me say this a hundred times, but it is good to remember this early: *Juries distrust lawyers who use tricks.* Today's juror has seen enough television, has read enough novels, and has watched enough legal thrillers

55

in the theatres that they know when a lawyer is trying to "gain control of the courtroom."

The person who should be in control of the courtroom is the judge. The jurors expect it, and if some attorney attempts to usurp that control, the jurors tend to resent it. The judge also tends to resent it. As do the clerks and the bailiffs.

Instead of trying to gain control of the courtroom, I would suggest the beginning lawyer take control of his or her case. As the stoic philosopher Epictetus would tell you, the only things in life you can control are your thoughts, your feelings, and your actions. All else is beyond your control, so don't stress about them.

How do you control your case? In a word, preparation.

First, you must know the facts. Sounds rather simple, but you'd be surprised how often a trial lawyer will walk into court barely understanding the detailed facts of a case. Usually in the civil context, everyone thought the case would settle, so the opposing lawyers are looking at one another with a mixture of confusion and fear, realizing that they are now riding a beast with many horns and legs and no sense of direction. The lawyer who knows the case inside and out has the upper hand from the outset.

Thoroughly read the file, talk to the client about what really happened, and do your investigation. Quite often, when you walk into court knowing what is good and bad about the case, you can literally scare the opposition into settling on your terms if they're not as prepared as you are.

Second, you must have a clean grasp of the case law and statutes affecting the case. This means that you do the research *before* you walk into the courtroom. You find the cases that go for and against you on matters of evidence and substantive law. You Shepardize them (oh, you'd be surprised how often busy lawyers leave the Shepardizing for the last minute, then forget to do it altogether). You make copies of the most important case.

I have seen lawyers who trundle into court knowing the issues, but having no idea of whether there is case law or statute on their issues. When the opposition has done its homework, they become the experts in that area of the law. Which side do you think the judge will begin to trust in argument? Or, for that matter, the jury?

Third, you have to plot your trial strategy before the trial. Know what you hope to accomplish with each witness, then stick to it. Understand the story you want the jury to hear about your side of the case, and what story the opposition will try to tell. Remember what evidence is important in helping your case, and which evidence is damning.

And, for heaven's sake, plan your cross examinations. We've all suffered through the purgatory of listening to an opposing lawyer who meanders through his or her cross because they haven't any idea of what they want to accomplish. We've all suffered the embarrassment for lawyers who have no idea of what they're asking or why, so they merely repeat what the witness said on direct. If you are fumbling for questions to ask, you're going to throw wild pitches.

Fourth, you should be on a first name basis with the evidence code and how it's going to apply to your case. If you're not surprised by an evidentiary issue, you anticipate what you will do when it arises. And you retain control.

Finally, you should remember that if you are surprised by anything, it is no shame to ask for a break in the action. There's no rush to keep the case rolling if the opposition springs a surprise witness on you. The judge won't beat you for asking to slow things down so that you can readjust yourself to new developments.

I was once surprised in the middle of a trial with an opposing lawyer who, as my client was about to take the stand, asked the court to allow her to reopen her case. She had witnesses, she said, who had heard me "coaching" my client fifteen minutes before he was to testify. (I had been going over his testimony, reminding him of things he had earlier told me.)

Turns out, these witnesses worked for her organization,

and weren't supposed to be listening in to the conversation between attorney and client. I asked for a break so I could look into this and, sure enough, there was a case that said that such misconduct on the part of the eavesdropper was grounds for dismissal of the case. When I brought this to the court's attention, the opposing lawyer suddenly decided that she wouldn't call the witnesses after all. Although I didn't get the dismissal I demanded, my client testified without harassment.

I felt gratified. I didn't even have to tap dance when we won the case.

SEE YOU IN COURT!

(FIVE WAYS TO MAKE SURE YOUR PROBLEMS TURN INTO A LAWSUIT)

Everybody says we live in a litigious society. The slightest little thing will land you in court. The smallest dispute will blow up into a major lawsuit.

But if you're a smart businessperson, you know this is not necessarily true. If you want to end up in court on a business dispute, you have to work hard at cutting off all other possible lines of resolution. People don't like going to court--getting into the witness box can make the dentist's chair seem like a vacation resort--and they'll do anything to stay out of a lawsuit. People don't like giving their hard-earned money to attorneys, either. If you like lawsuits, this attitude can present a problem.

While recognizing that there are simply some cases that have to be resolved outside of a courtroom, here is a guide to spurring suits for you hardy souls whose favorite expression is "See you in Court!"

1. BE UNETHICAL. Don't run your business with honesty. Don't try to provide quality services or products to your customers. You're in business to make money, not to make friends. Anyway, this city is so big that you can always find a replacement for the customer who shakes the dust of your establishment from his or her feet and swears never to return.

59

When some customer complains that you have not done what you were paid to do, or that a product you sold him or her is defective, that's their problem, not yours. Let them explain it to a judge. Most people won't bother--and you'll have a tidy little profit without the fuss of taking the time to provide quality services or products. And if they sue, so what? Even if they win, for every one that goes to court, you've made profit on five more who couldn't be bothered.

Of course, the lily-livered businesspeople will whine that providing quality service and products to the consumer is not only a good way to avoid lawsuits, it is also just plain good business. They'll tell you that when a customer has a complaint, you, as a businessperson, should take that complaint seriously and examine your own practices to make sure that you're not leaving a trail of unsatisfied customers.

But what do these people know? Sure, they've been in business for years, but chances are, they've never had the excitement of cross-examination, or that thrilling moment when the judge or jury renders their decision. Or, for that matter, the fun of avoiding judgment creditors.

2. BE UNREASONABLE. Do not, under any circumstances, tell the customer you will fix the product, render the service, or pay for any costs you caused. If you get into a dispute with a business associate or vendor, do not try to discover the root of the problem. In short, do not try to see the other person's side of the story. You are right and that's all there is to it.

When you begin to see the other person's side of the story, you will inevitably have to abandon the stronghold of your conviction that you are right, he or she is wrong, and there is nothing that can bridge that gap. Hold on to your position no matter what.

Some will call you unreasonable. Well, as someone once said, extremism in the defense of your business is no vice. (Okay, so that guy lost an election in a landslide. Big deal. At least he stuck to his guns.)

Even if you are wrong, do not admit it to anyone. Don't tell your spouse, your pet, your minister. Heck, if you're wrong, that's twice the reason to set your position in concrete. Once you admit you're wrong, you have to admit that you're liable--and that's a downhill slide. Instead, become doubly unreasonable. Retreat into the porcupine defense--roll yourself up into a ball and let them grab your quills. It's certain you'll end up in court.

So what if you get a reputation for being difficult to do business with? So what if people stop dealing with you because they know they'll end up in court with you? You can always move to another state and start over. And hey, there are 50 states out there--you won't cover all of them in your lifetime.

3. REFUSE TO NEGOTIATE. Negotiation is the tool of the devil. In the disguise of talking things out, you may actually find yourself agreeing to resolve the dispute for something less than full victory. You end up with no lawsuit. A good negotiation force everyone to settle for less.

So don't get suckered into negotiation. If you end up in a dispute with one of your vendors, don't let him or her convince you to meet to talk it over. All they want to do is convince you that they're right--after all, that's what you'd do. Heaven forbid that you'd ever have to admit that you were wrong about even the tiniest thing.

Wimps and weaklings, who are afraid of the consequences of their acts, will always cave in and try to find some middle ground. You, however, are better than that. When you negotiate, you will probably have to give up things. It doesn't matter that the other person will also have to give up some things. If you're right, why should you have to give up anything? If you're wrong--well, you'd rather hear it from a judge.

4. MAKE IT PERSONAL. It's especially fun to watch the expressions on your adversary's face when you drag his or her personal quirks into the dispute. For instance, when you get into trouble with that vendor who's been to the dessert tray once too many times, you can really score points by calling him a "lard bucket." If your opponent is a woman and you are a man, make sure you tell her that you think women have no business doing business. If you're a woman opposing a man, call him a sexist. If all else fails, fall back on such favorite ephitets as "liar," "cheat," "idiot," and "dog."

A well-timed insult can turn a minor problem into major litigation. When you inject personality disputes into a business dispute, you are sure to make the other party angrier, more intractable, and more prone to end up in court. They'll want to hurt you, and the way we hurt each other in America today is through the court system.

They'll want to make you pay big money for an attorney. They'll want to disrupt your business by the constant court dates and depositions. They'll want you to obesess over a long, ugly trial. They'll never stop to think that they will be involved with the same problems, spending the same kind of money, losing the same kind of time.

Again, the limp wristed approach would be to keep everything--even a bitter dispute--on a business footing. If an insult is raised by the other side, the white flag wavers would have you point out the inappropriateness of the personalizing of the dispute, and asking for a courteous apology. Then, they would say, proceed as if nothing happened.

But these are cowardly persons who don't know the joy of avenging an insult in court. If they'd been in charge of Tombstone instead of Wyatt Earp, there would have been no shootout. It would have become known as the "Settlement Agreement of the OK Corral." Where's the romance in that?

5. DON'T LISTEN TO YOUR LAWYER. Despite what you've seen on television and in the movies, not all lawyers want to litigate everything for you. Some of them are downright yellow, and will advise you to settle a case before the costs of suit get out of hand. Some of them will tell you that you don't have a good case and that the liability can be enormous unless you settle quickly. Some of them will tell you that your position is not supported by the law; that the facts are not in your favor; and that by filing a suit you'll be exposing yourself to a later lawsuit for malicious prosecution or abuse of process.

Some of these so-called lawyers will even analyze the problem for you and propose a mutually agreeable way out of the disagreement which will not only solve the problem, but will preserve the business relationship or the customer base for you. There are even a few who can help you avoid litigation altogether by setting up some procedures for your business which will prevent problems from happening.

These guys are panty-waists. They've got no fire in the belly, no grit or guts. They'd be happy to get your retainers and then do nothing but sit in their offices, telling you to stay out of court. They're not worthy of the name "Attorney at Law."

If you end up with one of these legal mice, fire him or her immediately. Go find yourself an attorney with a foxy secretary and a big, expensive office, who throws around phrases like "outrageous conduct," "million dollar verdict," and "sue the pants off these guys." Find an attorney who tells you that you don't have to take guff from anyone. Find an attorney who will be a pit bull, not a Chihuahua.

Then, sic 'em on your opponents. If you're lucky, your opponent will also hire a pit bull, and you'll have a nasty dog fight in court, complete with a red-faced judge yelling at both parties to behave. After all, what's the sense in going to court if you can't see a little blood flow between the attorneys?

These are only a few of the tactics you can employ in forcing your business dispute into litigation. The truly ambitious can dabble in the fertile fields of race discrimination, fraud, and double dealing. If you follow these tips, and make sure that you never put anything in writing, you are bound to end up in court two to four times a year. Then sit back and enjoy the show. After all, you've paid for it.

A Loss of Courtesy

What's the most worrisome trend in the business of law today?

To hear most older attorneys and some judges tell it, we are not threatened so much by the public's virulent hatred of all things lawyerly--nor that some will occasionally express that contempt with firearms; it's not the eroding resources of the courts to handle the double Stygian stables of ancient civil cases and crushingly complex criminal cases; it's not even the growing dissatisfaction which seems to drive the best and brightest minds away from a life in the law as if they were escaping a ravenous beast.

No, according to some venerable legal scholars, the major problem lawyers face today is what they euphemistically call "a loss of courtesy."

After reading some opinion pieces on the subject, I'm still not exactly sure what courtesy is being lost. Are we forgetting to say "please?" (*"Please don't give my client the maximum sentence, your honor."*)

Are we forgetting to say "Thank you?" (*"Thank you for completely gutting my case with that ruling on the evidence, your Honor."*)

Maybe we are being discourteous in our courtroom demeanor. Has there been a rash of attorneys putting their elbows on the table? Have some discourteous louts been taking their shoes off in court? Have we been leaving the courtroom without cleaning our plates and asking to be excused?

I don't know about you, but whenever a lawyer or judge brings up the word "courtesy," I tend to duck. It was a special pet for senior partners at big law firms when dealing with me when I was a lowly solo practitioner: *"Could you continue the deposition into the next decade so that my client won't be forced to lie under oath--as a professional courtesy?" "Could you convince your client to dismiss her discrimination complaint so that my corporate client can continue to keep women in their place--as a professional courtesy?"*

When a big firm lawyer uses the "c" word, he's got his hand in your client's pocket. When a judge uses it, there are often handcuffs involved:

"Counsel, if you don't begin to show more courtesy to the court, I'll find you in contempt."

"Of course, your honor. I don't know why I pointed out to you that your ruling on my motion to compel seems to be completely against all case law, statutes, common sense or decency. I don't know what gets into me, sometimes, citing cases at you. It's rude, and I should know better."[4]

---

[4]. Much as I don't want to be seen as copying the Hon Justice Bedsworth, a footnote is in order here. See *In Re Buckley* about one of our local legends who was cited for contempt for saying just such a thing.

Mind you, I'm not saying that lawyers couldn't use some sort of training in humane treatment of one's enemies. There should be a Geneva Convention to establish rules for litigators. Things like, you won't seduce the opposition's secretary to get inside information, you won't schedule an OSC on a day you know the other lawyer is going into surgery, you won't put a letter bomb in the envelope containing the answers to interrogatories. I know that at least two of these three things have happened to friends of mine.

But more often than not, those wise men who bemoan a lack of courtesy in the new lawyers are often more upset that no one rolls over and plays dead anymore.

As for myself, I resolve to be as courteous as I can-- within reason. I won't slurp my milk at depositions. I won't stick my fingers in my hears and hum during the prosecutor's final arguments. And I will never, ever call a judicial officer bad names until he's safely out of earshot.

My Addiction

So there I was in Barnes & Nobles, passing through on my way to get a coffee and an oatmeal cookie. It's dangerous for me to walk through a bookstore. What happens is pretty predictable.

Sure enough, as I'm passing the bargain book section, one catches my eye: *Learn Ancient Greek.* I pick it up and stroll through it (I was going to say peruse, but I learned today that peruse means to study carefully, not to stroll lightly). Yes, yes, this seems simple enough. A night a week, maybe a morning or a lunch hour. I'll be studying the *Illiad* in its original in no time.

After all, didn't Byron, Keats, Shakespeare, Frost, all those other guys who belong to that club to which I would love to claim membership—didn't they all study Greek? And Latin? And Aristotle in the original language?

I see another one: *The Great Philosophers.* It's a thin book, so should be easy to handle. I have been fascinated with philosophy even before I knew what it was. But there's another on heraldry. And there's one...

You see the problem. Like the ugly girl at the dance, I feel like I can't afford to say no. But if you were to come to my house, look in my car, visit my office, you'll see books all over the place. There are the Vietnamese tape and book I never got to. I was going to learn that language. There's the book on playing the electric guitar. I already play guitar but I knew this one would have some extra tips for me. There's the book called *Plato, not Prozac* on how to get yourself straight by dipping into philosophy.

I could go on. If a wise man always makes sure his grasp exceeds his reach, then I have to be the smartest mofo you'll ever come up against. My son's mother would say this is another sign that I have ADHD just as my boy does. And she'd likely be right.

But who has time for her? I'm still wondering about how difficult it would be to learn ancient Greek while still trying to turn the corner on Spanish, a language which I can now speak with halting basic fluency. It only took me twenty books and tapes to do so.

Aggression Pact

There are some trial attorneys who mask their incompetence with aggressiveness. You know the type: They bluster, they rage, they jump up and down, they yell, they mutter mysterious things about rights and justice and the unfairness to their client. Rarely do they deign to cite case law or statutes. Rarely are their arguments even coherent.

As lawyers, we seem to cherish the "quality" of aggressiveness, as if it were one of the seven heavenly virtues. When we describe an attorney as "aggressive," though, we are usually applying a euphemism for someone who is, frankly, a jerk.

The question is, do aggressive attorneys accomplish that much in court? When one is deciding on one's trial demeanor, can aggression win cases that otherwise will be lost?

What is called for is a definition, though definitions tend to be boring.

So: An "aggressive" attorney is one who not only is zealous in representation of his or her clients, but is obnoxiously so. The kind who say snide things about you to the judge, while you're standing there in open court. You want to turn and slap them upside the head but you know that, like with your parents, it will never be the instigator who gets punished. Or taken into custody.

An "aggressive" attorney is one who will refuse to give you the slightest room to answer discovery but who will wheedle and whine and mutter about "professional courtesy" when theirs is overdue.

An "aggressive" attorney will file a dozen motions, one after the other, so that you are so dizzy from answering their foolishness that (they think) you can't concentrate on getting your own case together.

An "aggressive" attorney will paper you with all kinds of discovery, including certain arcane devices which were popular at the time of Charles Dickens, and about which he wrote scathing novels. In fact, that's where they get their ideas.

An "aggressive" attorney is one who will push you to a specific trial date, refusing every single request you have for continuance...then, after you've subpeoned your witnesses and gathered your evidence and cleared your calendar to conduct the trial, will move for a continuance of their own on the day of hearing because they have a sick aunt somewhere who needs to be cared for. You will later discover that this lawyer has about twenty sick aunts, according to the other attorneys who have dealt with him.

Because in the end, most "aggressive" attorneys rarely go to trial. Why? Because the few times they went to trial they so aggravated the finder of fact—judge or jury—that they lost and lost badly.

In other words, a certified, gold-plated jerk.

This is what people look for, sadly, when they say they want a lawyer who will "fight for them." What they really mean is they want a lawyer who will put on a show of making life as unwieldy as possible for the other side, a lawyer who will bark and snarl at the opposition, a lawyer who will walk into court with a baseball bat and start swinging.

I wish I could tell you that these lawyers are unsuccessful fools, but more often than not they will get what they want because no one will want to deal with them long. And when two aggressive attorneys face each other in court, the blood will flow. And the judge will get a headache.

I am not an aggressive attorney. I have more respect for my blood pressure than to live constantly shouting and pushing and wheedling and snarking in court. I like to be as calm and as friendly as I can with the opposition. I find that it not only makes for a more pleasant legal life, but it also comes in handy on that rare occasion when you need a favor from your opponent.

And I have learned over the years how to handle the aggressive attorney. Much like you handle an aggressive dog. You bop them over the nose with a newspaper and tell them "no." Or you have the judge do it with sanctions or other such delicacies.

And you keep doing your job. Because the sole reason an aggressive attorney misbehaves is because he or she knows their case is terrible, their clients are at fault, and their own legal acumen is somewhat lacking. It's a ruse, much like certain wimpy animals in nature will bear their teeth when threatened. And while being eaten.

So, my friend, I recommend that you take the aggressive attorney in stride. Don't let them throw you off your game, don't let them rattle your confidence. Be confident in what you are doing and leave them to their petty games. The world sees them for what they are.

Father's Day

The man and his son sat in the front row, the bailiff hardly giving them a glance. It was the annual date for the court to approve of the son being at a board and care home for another year. The two of them had made this pilgrimage twenty-seven times since the son had been barely five feet tall. The son was now six feet, two hundred pounds. He was thirty seven years old.

The son was looking around anxiously, his eyes roving and flickering on first one object, then another. Sometimes he said something to his father in low, muffled tones, and his father answered in a deliberate, gravelly tone. The son stood up, made a circle with little steps, swayed. He tried to climb over the chairs at one point, but the old man's hand restrained him. The son was my client.

I went up to the two of them, shook hands with both, told them I was a Public Defender and that I would be representing the son today. The old man nodded his head. The son looked at me as if I were a dressed in the priestly vestments.

"How are you doing today, Jake?" I asked. He looked away from me, not meeting my gaze.

"Fine," he said in a forced, shaky tone.

"How are you doing in the board and care. Is everything okay there?"

"Sometimes they don't let me have my dinner," he said, staring at the floor.

"They don't? That's strange. They're usually very good about that sort of thing."

"They don't let me have my dinner," he repeated, then again, "They don't let me have my dinner."

The father, a gray-haired man with a square jaw, gently placed his hand on the son's elbow. The father wore an old denim work shirt, worn but clean. His eyes were steel gray.

"Jake, don't you mean they don't let you have dinner early?" the father prodded. Jake nodded, then repeated "They don't let me have my dinner."

"So you are getting fed okay, Jake?"

"Yeah, food's good." The words were a bit garbled, but I have learned over these last months to listen carefully to my clients.

The father then began asking me questions. How long would the judge's order stand? Could he still visit his son every day? What about bringing clothes to the facility? Were there going to be any changes? There had been a problem with making sure Jake could have a little money for personal care items, could something be done about this?

The questions were intelligent, hard questions, asked in a no-nonsense tone of voice.

"You visit him every day?" I asked at one point. The old man nodded, a bit puzzled that I would think such a thing strange. Many of my clients barely ever see anyone but the nursing staff and other patients. The family usually gives up, seeing the client once or twice a year--if that.

"So, Jake, are you all right at the facility other than not getting dinner early? Do you want to ask the judge for a change, or do you want to stay where you are?"

"Yeah, it's all fine, fine, fine," he said, a tremor in his voice. He turned around three times, as if looking for something. Then he sat down next to his father, and laid his head on the old man's chest. The father took his son's hand in his. With his other hand, he lovingly rubbed his son on the neck, on the shoulders, on the back. The son kissed his father's hand. Often my own seven-year-old son, when tired or nervous, will bury his head in my chest and hold my hand, for comfort and reassurance. I watched as the father kissed his thirty-seven year old son's forehead tenderly.

Here, I thought, was a child who would never grow

74

up, who would be in and out of facilities and board and care homes for the rest of his days. Here was a father who did not have the ability to care for a severely developmentally disabled person at home but who had still visited his child every day for twenty seven years.

I watched that stern-looking, gray-haired man who was unafraid to hold his son in that drab courtroom, and I wondered at how love must burn in him, undimmed over the years, knowing, as few of us know, the infinite capacity of a father's heart.

Standing Before the Judge

The trial has been lost. The client, who was full of bluster and indignation before trial, now looks like a dog that's been paddled with a newspaper. The prosecutor looks arrogantly at you both--but then, prosecutors pretty much always look arrogant. It's part of the job.

You stand with your client before the judge and your knees wobble a little. Hurriedly, you go over in your head everything you told the judge about the case before trial. Then you replay the sidebars. You wonder how many times you muttered Arockheaded idiot" under your breath as you came away from the sidebars, all of which seemed to result in the judge ruling against you. Big surprise there.

Now you are looking at the judge, who perches on his bench, one hand writing, one hand used as a cushion for his head. The old man looks tired but not worried. You both know that he knows already what he's going to do. Only one of you, however, knows what that actually is.

No slave caught stealing a grape from the Sultan's dinner ever quivered before that mighty fat-headed monarch with any more dread than you feel right now.

Still, it's your job to try to get the judge to understand your client's side of it--without arguing for his innocence, which will only infuriate the old bear. You want the judge to know that your guy's a family man, a working stiff, someone who needs to be out there contributing to society. In other words, all of the arguments this judge has heard a hundred times before from schills like you. You rack your brain for some new argument, but none comes. Facts are facts.

You wonder whether you shouldn't do a full-blown hearing. That's a defendant's right, isn't it? You can get family and friends and clergy to come in. Is the Pope going to be in town soon? You wonder whether you can ask for a continuance.

But when you look in the judge's eyes, you know it's useless. You could summon from the dead Ghandi, Mother Teresa, and John Wayne, and this judge would still impose a harsh, unjust sentence. He'd probably put Ghandi back in jail (though he'd let John Wayne off with a warning).

No, this dull-minded, spiteful, poor substitute for a judicial mind has already decided to max your client out. You see the prosecutor salivate.

You give your little pitch. This is just a misdemeanor. This is just an aberration in your client's life. There's no violence here, just a mistake--a mistake your client heartily regrets. You don't look at your client, but you hope he puts on the remorse heavily enough to be seen 100 yards away.

The prosecutor snidely recounds the facts of the case. Your client is a danger to society, he says. This is a serious case. Max him out.

When the judge gives your client probation and community service, at first you don't hear it. Was that an angel choir? Did a miracle just happen?

You walk out of the courtroom pleasantly stunned. Your client is talking about an appeal. But you've gained new respect for the wise man in the black robe who can see past your lawyering and understand that, as obnoxious as your client may be, he should only be punished for what he did, not for what he is.

Everything I Need To Know About Being a Lawyer I Learned from a Six-Year-Old

My six-year-old son, much to my joy, has shown a great aptitude for art and science. He will happily draw for hours and come up pictures of farm animals or jet planes which resemble the sort of thing Picasso was doing in his last years. Sometimes it will be pictures of jet planes strafing farm animals, but what are you gonna do? He can name the planets, a number of dinosaurs, and even tell a decent joke when prompted.

He is, in other words, a light to all who behold him, a comfort and joy to his old father, the golden child.

Which makes what happened recently all the more disturbing. Despite my best efforts to shield my son from his genetic heritage, I'm afraid that I am, after all, raising...a lawyer.

It happened in a toy store. His mother and I have not lived together in years, but we do cooperate in trying to make sure that what happens at mommy's house is pretty similar to what happens at daddy's house. With a few changes in the local rules for daddy's house.

His mother, for instance, did not want him to have any army toys, toy guns, or other implements of violence, even of the plastic variety. I, on the other hand, fondly remember the happy days of my childhood in which the neighbor kids and I would engage in elaborate and furious mock battles with plastic rifles, cap guns, sticks whittled to look like a laser, and anything else our evil little minds could conjure. It was fun. It was harmless. It was the type of thing little boys have been doing for seven thousand years.

So one of my local rules, which aren't reported in the Daily Journal, is that we can have certain "special" toys at Daddy's house. His mother finally relented and allowed him to have toy jet planes at her house, but she continually warned me not to introduce plastic toy soldiers into the mix.

One day the boy and I were at a toy store, and he became enamored with a package of 100 toy plastic soldiers. He had already been playing with some at his friends' houses, and he wanted to know if he get his own for his birthday.

"I'll think about it," I said, non-commitally, "but if I do get them for you, they have to be a daddy's house toy only. Mommy won't let them in her house."

"Why not?" he asked.

"She just won't. So if you get them for your birthday, you have to keep them at my house."

He thought for a moment, looking at the toys.

"Why doesn't mommy like toy soldiers?" he asked.

"It's because of the guns. Mommy won't let any toys with guns into her house."

"Well, I have toy jets at mommy's house, don't I?"

"Yes."

"And toy jets have guns, don't they?"

"Yes."

"And mommy lets me keep the jets at her house even though they have guns, doesn't she?"

"Yes."

"Then why wouldn't she let me have toy soldiers?"

Suddenly I was on the witness stand. And I didn't like where the questioning was going.

"Jets are different from the toy soldiers."

"What makes them different?"

"Well, toy soldiers are shaped like people."

"People fly jets, don't they?"

"Yes..."

"And in some of the jets, they put a little toy pilot to fly the jet."

"Yes."

"And the pilots of the jets look like people, just like toy soldiers look like people, don't they? It's kind of the same thing, right?"

"Yes. Sort of."

"So mommy won't mind if I have toy soldiers in her house, will she?"

I stood in the store helplessly. My son had just cross-examined me, and had done it better than some experienced trial lawyers I'd seen. I was worried. And it wasn't just that I knew that his toy soldiers would end up at his mother's house, nor that I had been bested by a six-year-old. What bothered me most was that my son was showing all the signs of becoming a lawyer. And I had *so* hoped that he would choose a profession that would make him happy.

Suddenly, his recent behavior became clear to me: How, whenever he would be asked why he did something he knew he wasn't supposed to do, his inevitable answer was "I don't remember." How, whenever he had to do his chores, he would always negotiate for something different-- not necessarily better, just different. How he was always late, and how he always had a damned good excuse for being late, usually an excuse that couldn't be verified. All he needed to do now was take the bar exam. He already had the rest of being a lawyer down cold.

I'm not sure, but I think I started to cry right there in the toy store. He looked at me with owlish concern.

"Daddy, are you all right?" he asked. Then I thought I heard him say, "*Maybe we should take a recess and resume questioning later.*"

"What did you say, son?"

"I said, let's go get an ice cream and I'll think about the toy soldiers."

"That's a good idea," I said. "Oh, and son, if you do get some toy soliders and you want to take them to mommy's house..."

"Uh huh?"

"How about if we let you talk to her about them? I have a feeling you'll have more luck with her than I ever will."

He now has toy soldiers at mommy's house *and* daddy's house. But from here on in, I'm hiding my law books from this kid. Toy soldiers are harmless; law books can be dangerous if they fall into the wrong hands.

What the Juror Thought

I thought they'd never call my name. That TV in the jury room is getting to me. If I see one more Ginsana commercial, I'm going postal. And who knew these soap operas were so annoying? Everyone is better looking than you are, and I'd love to have their problems--like which gorgeous person should I sleep with next?

Okay, who are these guys at the table? Must be the lawyers. At least one of them's dressed pretty well. Nice suit. The other guy must be a Public Defender. Looks like he got his suit at Goodwill. Hey, guy, discover the wonder of ironing.

Who's that guy on the other side without the tie? Must be the defendant. What an ugly guy. Wouldn't want to meet him after dark. I wonder what he did? Probably some horrible crime. They'll probably show me pictures that will give me nightmares. Man, he looks mean.

Here comes the judge. Kind of looks like Uncle Jim-- the one who used to pull on my ears and call me "squirt." I wonder where Uncle Jim is now. Is he dead? Or did mom say...

Uh oh, they're asking me a question. Can't remember what they said. Better say something.

"Of course I can be fair...No, I really don't know if the defendant is guilty or not...That would depend on the evidence."

Hey, I did that pretty good. Go ahead, ask me another. This is a little like Jeopardy. I'll take reasonable doubt for 300, Alex...

Oh, they're talking to someone else now. Boy, look at the defendant. He's glowering at me. I hope they don't tell him where I live. I'll probably be murdered in my bed.

What's this? I'm taking an oath? Oh, heck, they've picked me for this jury. Well, too late to back out now. I wonder if I should tell the judge that the prosecutor looks familiar to me. Isn't he the guy who cut me off this morning? Yeah, he is--the arrogant punk. I'm not going to believe a word this guy says.

On the other hand, he's pretty persuasive. Let's see. He's telling me the defendant was caught driving while he was drunk. Well, I don't like that. We'd better keep this guy off the streets. I wonder if there'll be any evidence.

Okay, the policewoman is on the stand. She looks nice in her uniform, very professional. The kind of cop you'd trust with your life. She keeps looking at us, too, like she knows what I'm thinking. Nice gal. Wonder if she'd be interested in my brother...

Who's this? The defense lawyer is asking her questions? Boy, he's pretty mean. Hey, he's really badgering this poor gal. Okay, so she got some details wrong--what's the big deal? what if her police report was wrong? Can't a person make a mistake?

Now who's this? The criminalist? What the hell is that? He did what to the blood? Man, this is really boring. Makes those Ginsana commercials seem exciting. I'd really like to get some sleep. I wonder if anyone would notice if I scrunched down and closed my eyes? Maybe it'll look like I'm taking notes.

What's that? We're taking a break? Did the criminalist finish? Did I snore?

Okay, in the hall. Let's find some coffee. Smile at the other jurors. God, what a homely bunch.

Bailiff's calling us back. I hope this gets interesting soon.

What's that? The case is over? Isn't the defendant going to testify? Doesn't he have to? What's he afraid of? I'll bet you he's so guilty he can't stand to look us in the eye.

Now the prosecutor is talking again. Yeah, yeah, we've heard it all before, guy. Hey, this schmuck is as

83

guilty as they come. Let's get this over with so you can go out and cut someone else off on the freeway, buddy.

Now the defense attorney's talking. This guy really annoys me. Reasonable doubt. Presumption of innocence. Who knows what all that means? Hey, I don't care if the cop got stuff wrong. She's obviously a stand up gal. Get off her case, already.

Now the prosecutor's talking again? Man, do these guys ever shut up?

Now the judge is talking. I can't understand a word this guy is saying. But he's still a dead ringer for Uncle Jim. Wonder where old Jim is now? I'd like to pull *his* ears.

What are they saying now? We've got to come back tomorrow? To do what? Deliberate? Why? This clown is obviously guilty, just look at him. I don't even want this guy out on the streets tonight. Let's take a vote in the box right here! Speedy justice, that's what I'm talking about.

Okay, I'll come back. What the heck--it's another day off work.

Maybe I should pick up some Ginsana on the way home.

The Blood Test

"I want a blood test," Jack said. "I can't be the father. I only slept with her once."

"Once can be enough," I reminded him.

Jack didn't want to be there, that much was obvious. I was a Public Defender in Orange County, on Dependency Court duty, and Jack had been dragged into a custody fight with the County over a daughter he didn't know he had.

Jack was 20, handsome and strong, but his job in construction was just a little above minimum wage. He had met a woman in a nightclub in those pre-AIDS days, had gone back to her apartment and had done what people did back then, without protection. Thus little Elizabeth came into being.

What Jack didn't know, what Elizabeth couldn't control, was that the woman liked cocaine and didn't know when to stop. Jack left the morning after and didn't bother to call—there was something about the woman he didn't quite like. Seven months later, Elizabeth slipped out of the womb, numb with cocaine.

Elizabeth's mother then disappeared from the hospital, one step ahead of social services and the police. But before she left, she named Jack as the father.

"I can't afford a kid," Jack said heatedly. "I live with my parents, for Pete's sake. I barely make ends meet now." Unspoken in the courtroom hallway was the added reason: Jack was young, good-looking, single. Who needed a kid to tie him down?

"Social Services says the girl is healthy and should be adopted pretty quickly," I said. "All you have to do is sign the adoption papers."

"I still want a blood test. Set a date," Jack said. I did.

On the appointed court date I ditty-bopped into the court officer's room with my stack of cases, intending to take care of Jack quickly. As dependency cases go, this was a simple one.

"Except your client didn't show up for the blood test," the County's court officer said, handing the adoption papers to me. "And he hasn't signed these yet, either." Great, I thought. Another flake.

I found Jack waiting for me in the hallway, sitting quietly on a bench. I sat next to him and handed him the paper.

"I'm not going to sign," he said.

"You didn't show up for the blood test."

"Don't need a blood test. One look at that kid and it's obvious that she's family."

"Either sign the adoption papers or you'll have to support her. Do you want the County billing you for her upkeep?"

"The County isn't going to raise her," he said. "I am."

That took me a second to absorb.

"They let me take her home last month," he continued, shaking his head. "Every night I was up three or four times, feeding her, changing her diaper. I don't go anywhere with my friends. I have to come home to Elizabeth. I probably won't go on a date for years. I don't have any extra money anymore. The kid cries a lot—I think that's because of the cocaine problem her momma had. It's really, really hard."

"Sign the adoption papers. You don't have to keep her."

"Yeah, I don't have to. But there's no way I'm going to let anyone else raise my daughter."

So we re-did the papers. Custody to the father. Case in Dependency Court dismissed. I came back to him, holding the pen out as he took the custody papers.

"This is your last chance," I said. "you can still back out."

"I know," he said as he signed.

86

Jack and Elizabeth never came back to Dependency Court, which is a good sign. I never heard from them again.

But I wonder about Jack and Elizabeth. What does he tell her about her mother? Does she know she could've been raised by strangers? Does she understand what her daddy sacrificed so that she could be raised by a blood parent?

I wonder if, like all little girls, Elizabeth believes her daddy is a hero.

I know I do.

Getting Clocked in Family Court

If the legal profession were an army, we all would have our roles. The public defenders and district attorney deputies would be the guys in the trenches. The civil attorneys would be the ones serving tea to the generals. Personal injury lawyers would be assault troops. Tax lawyers would be company clerks—the ones who always seem to have the nicest quarters, the best chow and the dullest jobs.

Then there are the ones who jump out of airplanes and hope that their parachute will open. You know, the guys that the rest of the army thinks are crazy—the divorce lawyers.

I have only dabbled twice or thrice in the fields of Family Law, a blessing which I attribute to a clean life and antipathy to figuring out the Dissomaster.

In fact, I had my fill of Family Law in my second case, one in which I spent far too much unbillable time arguing over the custody of a grandfather clock.

My client had been used to the finer things in life. She and her husband had traveled around the world, had driver Porsches and Cadillacs, had eaten at the best restaurants in Los Angeles. Their home was a showplace, with fashionable furniture and lots and lots of space.

When her husband one day calmly announced that he wanted a divorce, he hastened to add tht he would make sure that my client, who we will call Joanne, would not want for anything. After all, she had given him the best 15 years of her life, had borne his children, had not reported him to the IRS. She was due something.

Alas, his view of "something" and hers were wildly

divergent. She believed he was obligated to pay the mortgage on their 3000-square-foot house and pay her $10,000 in alimony each month. He believed that as long as she had a mobile home roof over her head and plenty of bologna to eat, life would be peaches.

By the time I got on the case (there were four other lawyers before me, and she was *in pro per* when she came to me), the courts were more inclined to his vision of her lifestyle rather than hers. All she had left was the white elephant of a house, for which she could not pay the mortgage, and a few items of furniture—including the clock.

While trying to hammer out a final settlement, hubby suddenly insisted that he wanted the grandfather clock as part of his share of the community property.

She broke down into tears when I told her the demand.

"He's just trying to get back at me. He knows I love that clock. He can't have it."

Angry letters went back and forth between hubby's attorney and me. There were a few telephone calls in which I was accused of being unprofessional and I, sad to say, accused my learned opponent of being childish. We were being sucked into the vortex of the clock.

One day, a motion to compel production of the clock arrived at my desk. I fired off, in four hours' time, a stinging response in which I cited case law dating back to the pioneer days of California and certain real property principles which were majestically embedded in the Magna Carta. His response sneered at my case law and cited some ancient divorce law from the Code of Hammarabi.

Meanwhile, I was fielding tearful calls from Joanne each day about whether her precious clock was doomed. I tried to mollify her, but she was uninterested in the Magna Carta.

At a certain point, the judge worked out joint custody for the clock. Hubby was to have it for a month, then return it to Joanne. But this fell through when hubby was snubbed at the door when he came to pick up the clock.

89

Joanne told him that the clock was away visiting relatives, or some such thing. I anxiously called Joanne to tell her that the judge had ordered her to give up the clock, and she cried some more.

"I love this clock more than life itself!" she said. "If I have to go to jail to protect it, I will."

"Protect it?"

"I know he's going to sell it. I can't bear that thought."

A few angry letters from hubby's lawyers and a visit to the judge later, and we were quivering on the brink of contempt. Then, suddenly, hubby seemed to tire of the game, offering a discount on the pittance of alimony due in exchange for his relinquishing all interest in the clock. Even though it cost her a few thousand dollars, Joanne jumped at the chance.

As we were signing the papers, I said to her that this was turning out to be an expensive timepiece.

"I hope it keeps damned good time," I said.

"Oh," Joanne said, "it fell over in the earthquake before we separated. It'll never tell time again."

Now all of the civil and criminal attorneys are thinking that I just made this story up. All the Family Law attorneys are shaking their heads and are saying, "I've got one that can top that."

Revenge of the Tax Nerds

In its time, the TV show *L.A. Law* did some pretty unbelievable things, but the most unbelievable of all was when Arnie, the tax specialist, asked if he could litigate a trial. "It'll be fun," Arnie told his partners.

There are three things wrong with this picture. First of all, as any good trial lawyer will tell you, trials are never "fun." They're exciting, frustrating, stimulating, exhausting, and can operate as an aphrodisiac if the right two people are on opposite sides of the aisle. But trials are never fun.

Second, the word "fun" is not in the tax lawyer's vocabulary, unless it is starting the word "fungible." The very thought that a tax lawyer might think that anything beyond the tax code updates was fun is foreign to everything I hold dear in this world.

Third, and most laughable, is the thought that a top-notch tax specialist would come down from the mountain and litigate any kind of a case, much less a garden variety contract dispute.

Tax lawyers have better things to do with their time— like make money. Lots and lots of money.

Oh, God, but they earn it. I have always believed that people are rewarded richly in this life for being fascinated with the things the rest of us know are necessary but find boring. Just ask an engineer. But tax lawyers take something that is crushingly boring and incomprehensible to start with—the tax code—and turn it into an arcane art, one practiced only by the most sage and knowledgeable of black arts practitioners.

And woe to that man or woman who gets into tax for the money but has neither the inclination nor the temperament for tax law. Within a month, such a sadly deluded person will be screaming in his cubicle, tossing the tax code about like confetti, muttering obscene imprecations to himself. They will put this person in a strait jacket and release him into something unchallenging, such as insurance defense. Even then, he or she will be scarred for life and may suddenly begin to shout tax regulations when confronted by stressful situations.

On the other hand, those who love numbers and rules and regulations, exceptions and exemptions, nooks and crannies and ifs, ands, buts, wherefores; those who find sentences of less than two thousand words uninteresting; those who wear gray not because it's expected but because gray is a damned good color, thank you very much—these men and women worship the tax code. It is their bible, their Shakespeare, their Hemingway. They find a song in the statutes, one that sings them safely through the rocks while other, lesser beings would be broken upon it. They have made their bargain and have kissed the sirens of the numbers.

I say, more power to them. I love being a trial lawyer, even though you would have to multiply my income by an exponential to equal the lowest tax lawyer's. But that's because I have the kind of job they make movies out of. Everybody who ever dreams of being a lawyer thinks, at least in passing, of standing in front of a jury on a big criminal case, the life or death of their client falling upon their own eloquence. Not too many dream of that dramatic moment when the right exemption which allows their client to claim their mistress as a necessary business expense pops into their heads.

But the funny thing is, I'll bet you I get the same thrill out of standing in front of that jury that a tax lawyer gets when that exemption comes, as if from heaven. In our way, each of us is divinely touched. One of us just happens to be able to afford a Maserati, that's all.

The Loneliness of the Long Distance Lawyer

Recently, I called my old friend Ron, who is one of the best solo practitioners in the Valley. Ron was that rare breed--he seemed to love flying solo.

But when I talked to him, he was talking about quitting the law and becoming a family therapist. Ron, mind you, is a successful lawyer, has his own little building, has a large and loyal clientele.

"But I'm getting very tired," he said. "I don't know how much longer I can keep everything in the air."

Which, of course, reminded me of my own days running my own practice. And why I quit to become a public servant. And why I still respect those brave souls who fly the flag of the law on their own.

Being a solo practitioner is like Charles Lindberg crossing the Atlantic: You're alone, there's no communication with the ground, and you're trying to will a flimsy bucket of bolts over thousands of miles of water, looking for a dry place to land.

And you're doing it because you want to.

The beauty and the tragedy of the solo practitioner is that you answer to no one except your client and Providence. There's no great organization to press your creativity into a pancake. Nor can you rely on its resources. There's no litigation partner who will throw a huge project at you at 4:30 p.m. on a Friday. But there's also no one there to guide you through your cases, to watch as he litigates, to bounce ideas off of.

There are no fellow associates who will drop by your office when you're in the middle of a motion to distract you with gossip, office politics, and the football pool. But there are also no fellow associates who will...you know.

To run a solo practice is to run a marathon that never ends. You work in the morning. You see clients in the afternoons. You work and see clients at night. They call you at 4 a.m. to tell you that they want you to go down to get their kid out of jail. It's not your first 4 a.m. call from a client, either. It won't be your last.

When you're solo, your clients own your time. To build your practice, you need to keep on their "A" list, so often you will spend an extra half hour on the phone with an old client--a half hour that every law firm would bill for but that you write off to customer relations. And there's also the heartbreak of hearing that the same client you spent half an hour with on the phone ended up going to a law firm anyway because they deluded him into believing he could win a dog case. You lost out because you told him the truth.

But you're solo because you want to be free to tell the truth, to turn down bad or questionable cases, to set your own rules and goals. You're solo because when you were with the law firm, the partners too often talked about billable hours and rarely asked, "What's best for the client?"

No matter how good you are, your clients have little sense of loyalty. And you see the sense in it: Law is no place for sentimentality. If another lawyer can do a better job, then your client should go there. But you still sit in your office and stare at your diploma and look at the messages on the clip from the problem children of your practice, each of them re-asking the same questions they've asked a hundred times. And you know you'll answer them again.

You feel isolated. You are the man or woman in the booth, cut off from life and human contact. You need someone to talk to, but if you called a fellow solo practitioner for lunch, chances are they would be too busy to see you today.

The ancient Greeks said, you must run the marathon by

yourself, and you must run it every step of the way. And when you have finished a great case that you have brought in alone, beating some huge law firm; when your victorious client is hinting that he wants to cut your fee because it wasn't such a hard case after all; when you close the file, look out the window and realize that you're missing your favorite television show, again, because no one else will pick up the slack if you let it drop--then you remember that old Greek line, with all of the heroism and foolishness it embraces. And you smile.

Then you pick up the next file, open it up, start writing. And you start running again.

Why I Defend *Those* People

I was talking to a woman prosecutor I knew when the conversation somehow fell into why I still with the Public Defender, after all these years.

"You should think about joining the good guys," she said with a smile that would make a man forsake religion, country, and his favorite NFL team on Sunday. Of course, I think that I'm *already* working for the good guys.

I get it all the time. Every defense lawyer does, deputy public defenders four times as much: "How can you defend *those* people? Rapists, murderers, child molesters. I can see representing someone you know is innocent, but how can you find it in your heart to work for someone who is *obviously* guilty?"

Over the years I've heard a few unsatisfying answers to this question by my colleagues. One said "We defend the Constitution and your rights as much as we defend the client." To some extent this is true, but I can't help feeling like this is somewhat of a cop-out, as if we have to somehow wrap ourselves in the flag as an excuse for soiling our hands with a petty thief. And the truth of the matter is most trials are not about the constitution (other than the right to have a trial and a lawyer) so much as they are about whether Johnny had a tenth of a gram of dope in his pocket when the nice police officer stopped him.

I've also heard it said that "We keep the system working. Without advocates, the whole right to jury trial breaks down." This is also true, but unsatisfying. The last thing any P.D. wants to be is an enabler for a system that routinely sends men and women away for long years in the penitentiary.

Being more of a storyteller than a philosopher, I

97

usually think not in abstract terms of the Constitution or justice so much as Rudy Pirelli[5].

Rudy was a long time con. This guy's rap sheet read like the first season of *Starsky and Hutch.* He'd pretty much done every drug and theft crime in the books. He was the kind of client DA's love to take to trial. He had "conviction" written all over him, literally: Tattoos snaked up his arms, down his neck, out through his chest and up to his chin. Vipers. Naked Women. Dragons. Swords. Knives and guns. He had a shaved head and a cold, dead look in his eye. He'd been in prison for more years than he'd been out--almost more years than he'd been alive. He was, to say the least, a client with limited jury appeal.

He had just finished a stretch at Chino when the DA discovered an old case filed against him for an auto theft he'd done a few months before going to prison. The case had not popped up when he plead to the felony that landed him in Chino, but some enterprising prosecutor had tracked it down when it came time for Rudy to be paroled.

So they brought Rudy back down to Orange County to face justice. If they had done this before he went to Chino, the worst that would have happened is that Rudy would have done a subordinate term of eight months, tops. Since his prison term was up, the ante was again raised to about three to six years, including three one-year enhancements for prison priors.

---

[5] Do I need to say, this is not his real name?

I was still young and naive. It seemed cruel to me to let a man get within an inch of getting out of prison, then hammering him with another six. I had heard of something called a *Martinez* motion, which said that the court should dismiss an old case if by the prosecutor's delay the client had lost a benefit--such as a subordinate term. I called our resident speedy trial goddess, who encouraged me to run the motion, although she warned me that all the DA had to show was some thin justification for the delay and we would lose the motion.

I explained all this to Rudy. "I don't know if this will work," I said, "but I might as well try it. We've got nothing to lose." Rudy nodded tightly. He'd probably heard those very words in every trial and motion he'd ever been through. He remained calm, passive, lips pursed tightly. He knew this was going nowhere. He wasn't going to get his hopes up. He knew that the system hated him, the judges hated him, the world hated him. He knew the DA usually won, the PD usually lost. It was a game he was familiar with.

When we got to the courtroom, the judge looked at Rudy, looked at the ill-fitting orange jail jumpsuit Rudy wore, looked at the tattoos that wrapped around Rudy's skin. When I was finished with my showing, the judge looked over at the prosecutor and said, "Well, what say the People?"

The prosecutor, who had beaten me in every trial we ever had together, said, "The People don't think the showing was sufficient for the motion."

"The court," the judge said, "finds that there has been a sufficient showing. The People can now show reasons for justifiable delay."

"The People don't think this is necessary," the prosecutor said. There was a pause.

"So the People have no evidence?"

"No, your honor."

The judge paused again. He looked again at Rudy, at his jumpsuit, at his tattoos.

"Fine," the judge said. "The motion is granted. The case is dismissed."

I didn't look at the prosecutor. I was too stunned to look at anyone.

"What just happened?" Rudy said in his tough-guy manner.

"The judge just granted our motion. The case is dismissed."

Rudy looked a little confused, then he seemed to catch a light.

"There's no hold on me?"

"Not if the case is dismissed."

"I can go home?"

He said the word *home* as if it were an ancient and sacred thing, something he had heard about but had not dared to believe in.

"Yes," I said, "You can go home."

Out of the corner of his eye, the one with the three tiny blue-green teardrops tattooed near the eyelash, a real, crystalline tear formed. He blinked. More tears came. He wiped his eyes. He looked away. He muttered, "Thanks."

A lot of people would say that all I did was release a criminal back to the streets where he could do more crimes. I'm not sure to this day what happened to Rudy. I like to believe that the human capacity for redemption is such that it's just as likely that he took a turn for the better when he walked out of the courtroom that day.

But the point is that he had the chance to make that choice. My job is trying to give people that chance. I can't think of a better thing to do with my life.

A Matter of Opinion

"Why don't you tell people that you're working for the Public Defender's Office?" a friend of mine asked me recently. "At the end of your column it says that you're a defense attorney, but it says nothing about where you work."

"Simple," I replied, "I don't want to cause Carl Holmes any more trouble than I already have."

It's true, friends. I specifically asked *Orange County Lawyer* to keep where I work vague so as to keep the head Public Defender from having to answer the hard questions from the Supervisors:

"So, Mr. Holmes, is it the policy of the Public Defender's Office to aggravate judges?"

"Tell me, Mr. Holmes, do all of your deputies view jurors as being inattentive?"

"Hey, Holmes, are you going to start hiring six-year-olds to do your cross examinations for you?"

To quote a former president--who *never* worked as a Public Defender--let's make one thing perfectly clear: The opinions expressed in this column are purely my own. They do not reflect the policy of the Public Defender's Office. In fact, I'm not even sure there *is* a policy of the Public Defender's Office, beyond the obvious ones of representing our clients to the best of our ability and not removing our clothing in public. When I speak in this little corner of the world, I speak only for myself. In fact, I'm fairly certain there are a few things I've already said in these columns that have caused no end of consternation among the higher-ups. And no, I'm not stupid enough to articulate those things at this time, thank you very much.

M.C. Bruce

Just imagine what would happen if I blithely placed the "Public Defender" label on my column each month. The layperson would think that this was the opinion of *every* deputy public defender-- a public relations nightmare. The organization would have to protect itself. Every column would have to pass through a rigorous inspection up the chain of command. First my supervisor; then her supervisor; then the #2 person in the office; finally, to my buddy Carl. Do you think a guy who supervises over 250 lawyers and staff, handling everything from Mental Health to Death Penalty Cases might have a few more important things to do than shepherd my sparkling prose to press? I know how bureaucracies work, even one as benevolent as the P.D. I was once in the Air Force. We did a little radio comedy show beloved by all of the enlisted persons on the tiny base at which I was stationed. Then someone mentioned to the base commander that the radio station--10 watts, I think it was--could be heard off base on a clear night. Suddenly we had to run every script by my detachment commander. Trying to explain comedy and satire to a career Air Force Colonel was roughly equivilent to teaching an elephant to ride a bicycle: You've heard it's been done, but you just can't figure out how.

My supervisors, of course, have a better sense of humor than my former commanding officer. They hired me, didn't they? Still, I can imagine how *legalistic* this column would read after being strained of every last vestige of potentially offensive or awkward material by the chain of command. It's not for nothing that the words *legal humor* tend to be mutually exclusive terms. My columns would end up sounding like a PIP circular.

So, friends and neighbors, understand: I love being a Public Defender. I am proud to be a Public Defender. I'm not trying to hide the fact that I'm a Public Defender. But the opinions expressed in this column are purely and completely my own. If you have a gripe, blame the undersigned. Don't call Carl. He's got a few other things on his mind.

A Perfect Flaw

It happened to me again today. I had handled some file in the middle of a day in which I was handling about twenty files (such is the lot of a public defender) when I made a mistake. Not a big one, mind you. Not a mistake that couldn't be corrected later on. But a mistake, nonetheless.

My supervisor, who sometimes regards me with the same affection one would have for a loyal but rather clumsy hound, showed me the error to me when the dust and smoke from the day had settled. "Just pointing it out for next time," she said lightly, and without blame. What I *heard*, of course, was *Why didn't you catch this the first time? How can you call yourself a lawyer if you make mistakes?*

Strange to say, but the law is one of the few professions in which even the smallest mistake is not tolerated. Baseball players who make millions a year can fail two out of three times; Quarterbacks with a completion rate around 60% are considered superstars; even accountants can occasionally forget to carry the two into the next column and we shrug and say, "you can't get 'em all."

But if you, as a lawyer, make even the smallest error, you feel it climb onto your back like a rude and flatulent elephant. You duck inside of your office with the lights out, staring at the walls, wondering how you ever got through law school. You replay the moment in which you made the fatal error again and again, in a twilight instant replay, and you hear the announcers in your head: *See where he trips here, Mel? There's really no excuse for a professional lawyer to fumble something like this. It makes you wonder how he got into the pros.* You shuffle through the files on your desk wondering what else you've bollixed. You want to call your mother, except you're pretty sure she wouldn't be terribly sympathetic. "You need to be more careful next time," she would likely say. "After all, this isn't yard work."

As lawyers, we are supposed to be trained to look for the devil in the details. Don't we suckle exactitude at birth? Don't we march out of law school with a steely look in our eyes, aware of every single detail to every single file we ever touch? Yet, looking back, I can't recall when in law school, exactly, we learned the need for perfection. Certainly not in the "issue spotting" exams, in which all we had to do was note that John was committing some tort or other, and probably committing a crime as well. Certainly not in class, where we stumbled through the facts of the cases we had read so that the professors could demonstrate how brilliant they were. And no one anointed me, upon passing the bar, with that holy oil which infused me with perfect light.

Still, we demand perfection out of lawyers. The amazing thing is how close many of us come to perfection. Public lawyers, such as PD's or DA's, handle an enormous caseload of deadly serious cases, and usually work these cases with an accuracy and completeness that would impress an engineer. Even when a mistake is made, only one in a million are costly to the client. But you can bet that the other 999,999 harmless mistakes prey upon the minds of those lawyers like an earwig burrowing into their brains.

Why do we put ourselves through this? Why do we obsess over something we know we'll never achieve? Part of it, I think is fear: We can't relax and *allow* ourselves to make mistakes because that leads to sloppiness, the bane of all lawyers. Once you get used to making mistakes, once you say to yourself, "It's only one case," you've taken the first step toward eventually handing in your bar card. Today's error may be harmless. Tomorrow's sloppy mistake could, literally, cost a client his life.

The other culprit here is the media. All of the lawyer heroes we have been given, both by the John Grishams of the fiction world, and the Gerry Spences in real life, seem to effortlessly flow into perfection, seem to constantly be prepared, aware, one step ahead of everyone else. Quick, name a famous mistake that Clarence Darrow committed. Or Perry Mason, for that matter.

And when a fictional lawyer does, God help him, screw up, the entire episode is built around what an idiot he must've been to not see that coming. Even the eventual denouement in which the lawyer "redeems" himself by turning the tables on a tricky adversary don't quite wash the nasty taste of non-perfection out of the mouth.

We will always aspire to perfection. Because we are humans (most of us, anyway; I'm not necessarily speaking to the Civil attorneys here), we will often fall a bit short. There is no answer, as most of life flows on despite our sins. The old stoic philosopher Epictetus said it best many years before even my boss earned her law degree: If you trip over a rock and fall down, do you stay on the ground and bemoan your fate? Or do you get up, dust yourself off, and start walking again?

I took the file from her, brought it into court later that week, and corrected the error. I tried to hold my head high while doing so, as if I'd meant it to happen like this all the time. Hey, everyone makes mistakes. But not everyone has to know when *you* make one.

Why Clerks Love Lawyers

I walked into my favorite courtroom and my favorite courtroom clerk, fully expecting a hero's welcome for a column I'd recently penned on their profession. She fixed me with the gaze she reserves for lawyers who give her things late in the day to file--the sort of glare that could turn anti-freeze to ice--and held up the article.

"I suppose you actually thought this was funny?" she asked. I stopped short, mumbled something about that darn evil twin of mine using my name to get into the *Orange County Lawyer* again, then gave her my best sheepish smile. It worked. I was sheared.

"I, I was just trying to tell the lawyers out there, in a humorous way, that the clerks have a very tough job and that lawyers shouldn't act like arrogant prigs to them."

She looked unconvinced.

"You think all we do around the courtroom is eat donuts and play solitaire," she said.

"Not true. You also put up with me."

"*That's* a job for which I should receive hazardous duty pay," she agreed blithely. Then she sighed. "And the sad thing is, you're only a small irritation in my day. All day there are lawyers coming in here, filing things late and asking me to stamp them with yesterday's date. Or they come in at 4:30 expecting to have an *ex parte* heard by a judge who's halfway to the golf course. Then they blame me for not nailing him to the bench. Or they saunter in like an alley cat full of bad fish and try to *flirt* with me--usually because they need a favor." She pushed a file into a bin. "For those lawyers, it's the fifth circle of Hades--into the pony, never to be seen by human eyes again. Serves them right for thinking that I'm stupid enough to fall for a little flattery."

"Absolutely," I said, making a mental note never to flirt with a clerk ever again.

"And then they come into my courtroom, take candy from my candy dish, and never offer to replace it. As if I'm a candy store or a bank teller."

"Or they'll run in demanding--demanding, mind you-- that I track down their file which was heard on a date they can't remember, with a case name they don't spell right, with a case number they usually get wrong by three digits-- and they want it in fifteen minutes because they're already late to be in L.A. And when I find it--and I *always* find it-- they usually ask me if I can use my 'power as a clerk' to fix something they broke on it so that their clients won't be mad at them."

"That's not the worst," another clerk chimed in, who had come to deliver a file, said. "Once I was clerking downtown for Judge Jackson in a civil trial. This one lawyer was a real pest. I kept after him to post the jury fees for three weeks before the trial. Every time I would see him, I would remind him that the fees needed to be posted. Every time he would hit his head in surprise and say, 'My secretary keeps forgetting to do that. I'll get on her case tonight.'

"So I decided, two days before the trial, to go right to the source. I called the man's secretary. I asked why she hadn't sent the fees. I could hear the exasperation in her voice when she said, 'He keeps blaming it on the court clerks--says they won't tell him how much it is.'"

"Oh," said the first clerk, "you're talking about B---."

"The very same. He did the same to you?"

"Pretty much. Except on the day of trial--after I'd been after him for weeks on the jury fees--I told the judge, while she was on the bench, that fees had not been posted. The lawyer slapped the side of his head and looked apologetic. 'Your honor,' he said, 'Your very capable clerk just informed me this morning we hadn't posted the fees. I'll get to them right away.'"

"Please tell me he lost his case," I said, hoping for some confirmation of Karma.

"Sorry," the first clerk said, "he won hands down. And he and I had been arguing the whole time. When the trial was done, he sent a letter to my supervisor."

"What?"

"Yes, and he said that I was the most professional, courteous, and capable clerk he had ever dealt with. What he didn't say was that I didn't let him get away with one darn thing in the courtroom."

"At least he had the sense to try to get on your good side for the future," I said.

"He didn't get to be successful by being dumb," she agreed, putting my little article in her desk drawer. "By the way, all of your cases have been continued to 4:30 this afternoon. By order of the clerk."

"*What?* It's only 9:30!"

She flashed a Cheshire smile and closed the desk drawer.

"Gotcha," she said, as the judge came out. He had my files in his hands. "Be careful what you write in the future," she said. "You never know when you'll meet up with someone who's less understanding than me."

Catching the Small Fish

I've just come from court where my client received four years in state prison for possessing half a gram of methamphetamine. That's not even enough meth to cover the bottom of a bottle cap.

The judge was quite clear when sentencing him: He was being sent to state prison as much for his four-year-old armed robbery as for his present case.

This is a scene replayed in court after court in California since the passing of the three strikes law. If a defendant has even one "serious" felony in his or her past, a new felony, even a non-violent self-destructive felony such as possession of methamphetamine, means no probation, double the prison term. Although the California Supreme Court ruled a few years ago that judges have the power to dismiss such priors, most judges are reluctant to do so, given the present political climate.

I am a firm believer that our society will eventually be judged by the fairness of our law, the wisdom of our justice. And I have no doubt that someday our day-to-day use of the three strikes law to imprison addicts will be considered with the same disdain and horror that we have for the laws of 17th Century England, where a shoplifter could be hung for his second offense.

Our three strikes law began with the ugly, tragic killing of Polly Klaas. Her killer was a parolee, out of prison despite a long record of violent crime. Had there been a three strikes law then, Polly would be alive today. You'll get no argument from me on that.

But I worry about a law aimed at violent, dangerous people, like Polly's killer, which seems to more often trap pitiable drug addicts trying to feed a ravenous addiction. I worry about laws aimed at making our streets safe that have the ultimate effect of warehousing in prison young black and Latino men--the overwhelming number of strikers tend to fall into these groups--usually for crimes which are annoying and undesirable, but a far cry from the violence we all fear.

A "strike" is not merely a killing or a robbery. A strike in California can be a residential burglary--if someone breaks into your garage and steals a bicycle tire, and your garage is attached to your house, it's legally a residential burglary. Would that defendant be so dangerous to the community that we need to lock him up for a minimum of 32 years when he comes through the system years later for possessing a tenth of a gram of heroin?

For most people the answer, evidently, is yes. To do less would be considered to be coddling a criminal. To try to address the root of the defendant's problem, his addiction to a controlled substance, is seen as limp-wristed liberalism.

When did we become so angry? When did this stop being punishment and start being vindictive? This is an attitude which was brewing long before Polly Klaas, long before the OJ trial, even long before Charles Manson. The public believed that the crime rates were rising because the courts were being soft on crime. It was a slam dunk for politicians to argue for tougher sentencing laws. Never mind that much of crime could be traced to stiff economic problems, overcrowding in the cities, disaffected ethnic minorities being pushed down by a clueless majority.

Recently, when there was a drop in crime, prosecutors and police were quick to credit the three strikes law. But crime is down all over the country, even in states where there is no three strikes law. The economy is good, minorities are on the rise into the middle class.

No matter. We have lost our perspective. We no longer make the punishment Afit the crime," but seem to thrill in punishing every criminal harshly, no matter what kind of crime he's done.

I keep thinking about my addicted client, who will spend the next four years in a prison, where drugs are easily obtained. When he gets out, I'm sure he'll be arrested again for attempting to poison himself with methamphetamine. Or maybe he'll try to steal something to support his habit and get caught. Then he'll do another five, maybe six years in prison.

To many, that's not a tragedy. In fact, I'm sure there are some who will read this and say "Good. He gets what he deserves, the lousy drug addict. Let's keep him off the street."

My fear is that, eventually, we will also receive what our vindictive sentencing laws have reaped for us. In the end, our harsh laws may end up hardening him into a lifetime career in crime--and in prison. I'm not sure whether his fate will be a judgment on him or a judgment on us.

My Dinner With God

The e-mail had been forwarded to me by my Aunt Elva. She was a high school principal in her time, though she's retired and in her 70s now. She belongs to that generation which accepted the homogenized version of God unthinkingly. Now she, and those like her, is appalled at how godless society has become.

She had just forwarded me an e-mail that purported to be a "true" story about how a godless set of parents had killed themselves on drugs and violence in front of their little girl, who was "protected" by an unseen presence which she later tells a Sunday School teacher was the exact man who is portrayed on the church wall as Jesus. This "true" story is actually a fictionalized country song which was popular about a year ago, but this is how the internet works: Someone decides they're going to fudge the facts a little in service of the Lord, even if it means slipping on one of those pesky Ten Commandments.

This particular e-mail, however, really got my goat. It purported to be a transcript of an interview with Billy Graham's daughter, who was asked how God could have allowed the attacks of Sept. 11 to happen. Instead of talking about Middle Eastern politics, or of how Americans are perceived in Arabic countries due to long standing foreign policy, Ms. Graham is reported in the e-mail to have blamed the removal of the Ten Commandments from the schools; the rule against reading the bible in public schools; the hedonistic attitude of Hollywood toward sex and drugs; and a few other pet peeves of the religious right. "We have turned our backs on God," she is reported to have said. "Is it any wonder God turns his back on us?"

This argument has a certain sentimental and emotional appeal to those who see our "morals" slipping. The unstated argument is, bring back God to the government, and God will be nice to us again.

Now, I believe in God. I think I have a pretty good relationship with Him. I'm a good person, I try to do good in this world, I try to be honest, I try to instill these values in my child. I am not much of a church goer, but when I do, like my Aunt Elva, I attend Roman Catholic services. Unlike my Aunt Elva, I'm willing to admit that we Catholics don't have a monopoly on the "true" religion. I like to think that God is a little more broad minded.

I refuse to subscribe to the "God is mad at us" version of modern life. I, for one, refuse to believe in a God who is as petty and small minded as I am. I like to think that the things that have happened, though traumatic, are nothing worse than other terrible things that have happened from the dawn of time. You can go to any century and find atrocities or natural disasters, even in the most God-fearing of lands. Renaissance London was full of believers. Still, they had a great fire. Roanoke was a colony in the new world founded by very pious people. It disappeared without a trace. The Holy Roman Empire had to face down first Attila the Hun, then other barbarians, and eventually was broken apart.

Even in our time religiosity is no guarantee that you will be safe. The newspapers are replete with madmen stepping into churches and killing indiscriminately; with religious fanatics of one brand of the world's one true religion slaughtering women and children of another one true religion, just to show their fanaticism. For that matter, the Sept. 11 attacks were made by men who believe they were doing God's will.

Therefore, I am very leery when any human begins to tell me what's on God's mind. Or why He's "let" so many things happen to us. To believe this is just another way of abdicating responsibility for our own actions, or those of other humans.

The religious right, however, has a vested interest in bringing God back to the schools and other areas of public life. To them it is a power struggle. If they succeed, due to such emotional pap as the "true story" that turns out to be a fictionalized country song, or the "God has turned his back on us" dodge, it will enhance only their own temporal power. God will be neither stronger nor weaker than before. Hey, let's face it. If God is a billionth as powerful as we should believe Him to be, being God and all, He doesn't much *need* us, nor our schools, nor our government.

I think, in fact, He would view our fellow humans' attempt to divine what's wrong with Him with some amusement. I'd forward the e-mails to him with a funny comment, but God doesn't seem to be on the net. Has He turned his back on the Net?

Abe Lincoln and Me

As lawyers, we have our own heroes. By and large, though, they are people rarely known to the general public. We idealize men like Felix Frankfurter (whom the man on the street would assume was the creator of the hot dog) and Benjamin Cardozo. We remember The Great Dissenter (Justice Oliver Wendell Holmes) and Earl Warren.

But one lawyer hero that is instantly recognizable is Abe Lincoln. When people remember Honest Abe, though, they rarely remember that he was a lawyer. Most of them think of him as the bearded guy who fought the Civil War barehanded and whupped the Rebels in a brief four years.

I don't flatter myself that I am simpatico with Honest Abe. Still, many of the things he believed in are things I have tried to put into practice myself.

Abe was a solo practitioner much of the time, or in partnership with his friend Herndon. He never worked for a big law firm or the DA's office. He stayed small time even when the railroads hired him for civil stuff, even when the businessmen of Springfield began to use his legal acumen and pay him nice fees. He never got too big for his britches. He remembered that the reason he wanted to be a lawyer in the first place was not merely to make money but to help people. So when an old widowed friend of his begged him to defend her son in a murder case, Abe did not say "call my secretary" or "how much money have you got?" He said yes, won the case (it was the famous "moonlight" case) and then refused to take a penny in fees.

I like to think that Abe would have been proud of me the time I got a call from a single mother, aged 17, who told me that she desperately needed a lawyer in family court but could only pay $100. I went ahead and said yes despite the fact that we were talking about thirty hours' work, because the girl needed help and there was no one else. It was a bonus, of course, when she finally came to sign the contract in my office and I discovered that she was gorgeous and sweet and fierce.

Abe was not a shark. The story is told that two farmers he knew both consulted him about a lawsuit they had against one another. Abe didn't take a large fee from either; instead he called them both into his office at the same time and negotiated a settlement of the dispute which restored good feeling between the men.

I tell my family law clients that resolving short of hearing is always better than putting it in front of the judge. In one case I had an *in pro per* father on the other side, and he had made some unfortunate errors in his preparation for hearing. Instead of taking advantage of the errors, I told my client that her child would be happier if she were able to work out visitation details with Dad. This saved the child from coming to court. A settlement was worked out and I did not have to feel like a snake by pounding the father for his inability to navigate the legal system.

Old Abe used to wear a stove pipe hat so that he could keep legal documents in there. The story is told that once in the middle of a hearing, he pulled out his hat to produce the crucial contract that won his case.

I don't wear a hat, but I do carry around a bulging briefcase which I like to refer to as "my bag of tricks." If you were to look in there, you would be stumped to find anything resembling organization in the bag. All too often, I am stumped as well.

Abe liked to tell funny stories to illustrate his points to a jury. To bring home that one witness was a calculated liar, Lincoln told the jury that he was like a rabbit: He'd go into one hole and pop out of another.

I love the funny story. I once had a case in which the cops had busted my guy for giving them a false name during a warrant search. My guy happened to pop onto the scene because his car broke down and some guy in a t-shirt asked who he was. My client, suspicious as to why a white

116

guy needed to know his name, naturally gave a false one. That's when the t-shirt guy showed him a badge and my guy told him the real name. Nonetheless, the DA filed.

I told the jury about when my artist father, who loved to paint rural scenes even though he had grown up in the city, found this picturesque piece of farm equipment rusting at the side of the road and painted it, an angry sky as background. He called it "Storm's a-comin'" and exhibited it at a rural art show in California. At the show this farmer stood in dirty overalls looking at the picture and smiling.

"Like the picture?" my dad said, sensing a sale.

"Sure. It's the prettiest picture of a manure spreader I've ever seen."

The case, I told the jury, is just like that picture. The Cops and DA think my guy was up to something no good, and so they charged him with a foolish crime. But, in truth, all they had was a manure spreader.

The jury laughed. And acquitted.

Abe believed that, despite the lawyer's reputation, attorneys needed to deal with one another honestly and with courtesy. You can oppose one another vigorously in court, he said, but when it was over you should be able to go to the local tavern and share a drink. It should never be personal.

I admit I fall on this more often than not. I have a case against another lawyer who recently filed with the county a document which I demonstrated to him was completely illegal. This lawyer tried to wriggle out of the case law and statutes I cited but he and I both know he is just doing this illegal thing to get a leg up in the litigation. I find it hard to be courteous to such a person. I hope Abe will forgive me.

Della Street and Me

Years ago when I first started my solo practice, I read the bible on starting such a practice by Jay Foonberg. On the Subject of hiring a secretary, he noted that Perry Mason had Della Street to help him and she always knew everything: When he was supposed to be in court, when he was supposed to file motions, when he hadn't eaten for two days, when a client was going to be arrested. For good measure, she helped him solve a few thorny cases.

Then came Jay's advice: "Hire Della Street."

I can't tell you how often I have rued not following his advice.

You see, young lawyer, I opened my solo practice after years as a public defender. I had also worked for a large civil firm for a few years. I can type at 125 words a minute and I find that often I write better motions when I write directly on the word processor.

So I thought I didn't need Della Street. How hard can it be to file papers? Keep track of my schedule? Remember to eat every few days?

Alas, the only thing I never missed was the eating every few days. It has become apparent as my practice has stumbled along that I should have hired Della Street from the start, no matter what the cost.

The first sign came when I missed a deadline to file a response to a motion. I had to go through several gyrations to get an order shortening time, something that sucked down about three hours. Three hours I couldn't, in good conscience, bill the client for, as it was my own damned fault for not remembering the deadline.

Then came the call from Department 5. Where are you? You were supposed to be here for the pretrial on a felony case at 2. Now it's 4 and everyone else has gone home. We're trailing this for a day but you'd damned well better be there tomorrow.

Then came a call about a document which should have been easy to track down. After all, I was doing my own filing, wasn't I? So I dove into the stack of things that were going to be filed "as soon as I had a spare moment." Not there. I looked in the file. Not there, of course. I looked under my desk. In my car. In my bedroom. I asked if I had left it in court. I looked everywhere for the damned thing before I had to call the client in humiliation to tell him that I could not locate the damned thing anywhere. This is, by the way, why I tell my clients NEVER to give me the original of their documents.

After going through the predictable conversation with the client about what a terrible lawyer I must be because I can't keep track of documents, we were able to recreate the document—another three hours gone that I would not bill the client for because I don't have that kind of toxic audacity.

Okay, I would tell myself after each problem. I am going to get on top of this stuff. I am going to make sure I don't miss deadlines by having a tickler file. I am going to redouble my efforts to keep two calendars so that I don't miss appearances. I am going to file every document as I get it, and not create a stack.

All good resolutions. But I forgot one minor detail: I am a lawyer. I have 100 things to do even on a slow day. All of those things seem to be more urgent than filing or maintaining my calendar. And though all of the lawyer things got done, I was more and more getting burned by my failure to remember deadlines, to schedule appearances, to file documents.

The worst of it came one night when I finally sat down to file an appeal on a felony case which I had promised the client would be done with dispatch. When I finally looked at the date I realized I was a week late for filing the appeal.

Appeals, for those of you who blessedly have never had to deal with them, are as unforgiving as a cat. If you blow a deadline, the appeals court accepts no excuse. None. Malpractice, baby. Turn in your bar card right now.

The thing that saved me was my lawyer acumen— instead of throwing in the towel, I researched and found out that on felony cases, *and only felony cases*, you can tell the court that your client wanted an appeal, told you he wanted an appeal, and it is your own damned fault and no one else's that it didn't get filed in time, and the court will accept that and let the appeal be filed.

But this was too close for comfort. Malpractice was right around the corner.

You see, young lawyer, you will be so wrapped up in the law and the client's case that little details will escape your notice. You will think that you can easily file things with the clerk—and you can—but what you will forget is that such things can take an hour or two out of your day.

And let's face it: There are no law school classes in how to be a legal secretary, and with good reason. You have to be really smart to be a legal secretary. You have to have your ducks in a row and your decoys lined up. You have to be organized. All of the things a good lawyer never is.

The worst thing is that being a Legal Secretary is a full time job. It takes a lot of brainpower to be one. When you run your own practice and act as your own legal secretary, you are doing two very difficult jobs. You will find that the lawyering is the easier of the two.

So I asked my lovely fiancée to become Della Street. She used to be a school teacher, so she is used to unruly and foolish children such as myself. She now does my filing. My scheduling. My tickler file. And life is easier.

Though not quite as easy as it would be if I had only hired Della Street to begin with.

Making it Look Easy

O, Lawyer, you work hard in your practice. You work long nights researching an obscure point of law when you know your opponent is watching *The Daily Show.* You spend early mornings poring over depositions and other transcripts to find that one little gem which will drop like a nuclear bomb during trial. You read police reports as if they were holy writ on your so-called lunch hour because you are certain that the cop betrayed himself when describing his probable cause to stop your client and you want to suppress the evidence.

Then you walk into court, as prepared as a human being can be…oh, sorry. Prepared as a *lawyer* can be. You have your notes, your post-it riddled transcript, your scrawled case citations with the quotes from great judges.

The moment comes. The witness is on the stand and she is blithely lying out of her capped teeth. She's saying she never, in a hundred years, knew that anyone had ordered the software for the corporation, and that's why she called your client's employers to tell them that she thinks he had pirated that software from their business. She doesn't care that he got fired from that lie. She is telling the jury that it's not a lie, that she honestly thought that this software had been pirated because someone told her so and she had no idea that it had been legitimately purchased.

And you are ready, aren't you? First, you pull out her deposition. She said the same thing at the depo, and you marry her to the statement. Not only do you marry her to it, you send her on a honeymoon with that statement and set her and that statement up in a little cottage with a picket fence. She looks smug as you repeat the lie again and again. As does the opposing lawyer, a guy who is getting paid too much by a big law firm to squash your client like a bug.

And as the smugness in the room becomes so thick that you begin to choke on it, you go back to your desk. You are nonchalant. You are calm. With all the grace of a high-class magician, you produce the fatal document. You hold it in your hand. You study it in front of the jury without telling them what it is. The witness looks at you as if you are losing your mind. The opposing counsel, though, senses something is wrong. He begins to flip through his stack of documents, his exhibits, your copies of exhibits, the discovery. You are gratified to sense his desperation.

Innocently, you ask the question one more time. At this point the witness and her lie have had two children and a dog in that cottage and she couldn't deny she said it if she were suddenly to whip off her mask *ala Mission Impossible* and reveal herself to be Peter Graves.

Sure, she says, now a little uneasy herself, looking at the desperate look on her lawyer's face. Sure, she had no idea the software had been legally purchased before calling your client's employer and getting him fired for piracy.

You show the document to your opponent. The very sick and defeated look on his face is worth every dollar you spent getting your J.D.

You show the document to the witness, the one you found at 2 a.m. this morning, the one you vaguely remembered seeing in discovery from the other side, the one that somehow no one has noticed until now.

"This is an invoice from your company, isn't it?" Yes, she says.

"This is your signature, isn't it?" Yes, she says even more warily.

"And this is an invoice for the supposedly pirated software, showing that your company bought this software, correct?" Yes, she says, but adds that after they realized the software had been pirated they bought a legitimate copy.

"Could you read me the date which is on the invoice in your own handwriting?"

She looks. She looks harder. She looks even harder.

"It's dated two days before you called my client's employer, correct?"

Gulp.

The jury comes back with a $400,000.00 verdict for your client. The prior offer from the defendant to settle was $5000.

You are walking down the steps gratified, sure that your client appreciates what you have done to restore his good name, to win a big verdict in his favor. Then he stuns you by asking:

"You think you could reduce your fee a little?"

You adjust your ears to make sure you heard that right.

"Come on," he says. "This was an easy case for you. It was obvious to everyone she was lying. And that document was so blatant, no one could have missed it." You are too stunned to point out to him that *he* never noticed it while going through the documents. "So how about giving me a break on the price?"

And you realize again that you are a victim of your own legerdemain. You have pulled the rabbit from the hat and your client fully expected you to. You work hard to make it look easy. But, as always, all the client sees is the easy part.

The Lawyer as Human Being

I realize I might just as well have named this little essay "The cockroach as humanitarian" but please hang with me, friends.

Every day the lawyer faces a thousand choices. His or her first choice, of course, should be to serve the client ethically and with vigor, even if it causes dismay and gnashing of teeth for his or her opponent. In fact, most lawyers I know enjoy their jobs most when they cause dismay and gnashing of teeth to their opponents.

But one does not have to be a pit bull to be an effective lawyer. I have often had the upper hand in a case but recognized that my client would be better served by settling than by a smashing victory. This is especially true in family law court, where the stakes are as high as they will ever be, outside of Capital Cases.

One family law attorney I know has used his skill and acumen in that field to consistently deprive one party of their children. In a case which I fought tooth and nail, my client suffered from clinical depression. As is the problem with such people, she refused to believe it. This attorney, knowing that her relationship with her children was the only thing keeping this woman on this side of sanity, worked diligently first to force her into supervised visits, then to completely eliminate visits with her children completely. It didn't help that I thought his client was a psychopath who was trying to punish my client for ever having the temerity to be in love with him in the first place. I was sure this man was using his lawyer as a weapon to drive my poor client over the edge.

This lawyer eventually won, convincing a judge that a woman who had never been a threat to anyone would somehow explode into crazed violence unless she was properly diagnosed and put under medication. He knew she had no money (I had been retained by a friend and ended up doing 90% of the case *pro bono*) and that to get such a diagnosis would cost her $2000. Now, if this lawyer's gainfully employed client were offering to pay for the diagnosis, that would be one thing. But this guy wanted to see her suffer and he would not pay for it. Nor would the judge order this, despite my pleas that the judge was illegally depriving her of her children without due process.

I see this woman, still, walking the sidewalks of my town. She is always sad. Always angry. Still depressed. Still not seeing her children.

I once saw the psychopath walk into a coffee shop with one of his children. The girl looked guarded, haunted, sad.

I wonder about this lawyer. He is a smart man. I am sure he knows that his client is not Prince Charming. I am sure because I have occasionally had clients who were evil and I found a way to do well in the case without doing evil as well.

But this guy—and he's terribly successful—has not a second thought about how he is ruining the lives of my client and her daughters. In fact, he likely boasts of it at night to his empty house and his angry dogs.

I do notice, however, that this man seems to walk this world with a permanent scowl. He rarely smiles—and that when he has scored a devastating point against a weeping mother in court. The man seems to have no fun. When he talks about his weekend, it's usually about how he went into the office to finish some motion. Is there joy in his life?

I use him as a test to myself. If I ever get to the point where winning the case is more important to me than helping my client's life, or if I ever value the fees that could be earned over the evil that I might do, I know that I will have to withdraw from this profession.

It is so easy to lose one's humanity in this profession. We are akin to Samurai, Japanese knights highly skilled at combat who would hire themselves out to different Lords without care for what they stood for or what oppression the Lord intended by going to battle. We tell ourselves that the way the system works is that we advocate to the best of our ability and the truth will eventually emerge, but any good lawyer will tell you this is nonsense. The alleged truth seems to favor that side which has the money for the experts and the paralegals and the high priced lawyers.

So as a lawyer, you have a choice. You can be a Samurai and hope that you hire on with a Lord who is benevolent and good hearted. You can hope that when that corporation hires you to convince a court that the toxic waste dump they have created is actually a jobs center for the community, or that its spillage into the local drinking water was all done in strict accordance with the law and therefore there should be no penalty.

If you don't do it, another lawyer will, you say. And you are absolutely right.

But that other lawyer isn't you. You can choose to try to use your legal acumen to help people in this world. Yeah, you will likely not make millions of dollars in fees, will not attract the big clients, will not win awards from the local bar association or have a big house and an expensive car.

But you will sleep at night. My colleague who knowingly deprived my client of her kids—well, that guy always has dark circles under his eyes. He's always cranky. I would not, for all the big fees in the world, agree to be afflicted with his nightmares.

The Missing Document

There are those who think that the Bermuda Triangle, in which planes and ships and other large objects have disappeared, is a mystery. I understand it perfectly. I am a lawyer and I have been entrusted with important documents. Documents which I knew I had to keep track of. Documents I treated with respect and care and attention. Documents which disappeared inexplicably, calling my reason for being into question.

The Missing Document. It is the bane of every lawyer's existence, no matter what you practice. Did you client give you the only copy of the deed to his property? I promise you, it will disappear. Did the client give you the handwritten letter from the other party admitting his total liability for the accident? Vanished. Did you find, after long hours of investigation, the name and address of that one witness who will completely change the case? You wrote it on paper? You fool! You might as well have written it on the wind.

I have worked for the best Public Defender's Office in the country, in Orange County. I have worked for a big law firm in downtown LA in which the lawyers charged $500 per hour for their services. I have been involved in court services and in arbitrations and in other quasi-judicial venues. The one thing they all have in common with my little law practice? In every office, documents have vanished like Houdini in handcuffs. Now you see it. Now you don't. And you never will again.

No one can explain how this happens. In medieval times the lawyers probably blamed it on demons. In WWII it was gremlins. Today we blame the computer.

But deep inside we all know who is to blame: The stupid lawyer. The one who does not take the document and immediately roll down to the bank and enshrine it into his or her safety deposit box. The one who does not frame the document and place it on the wall for all to see. The one who does not send it to his mother whom, we all agree, has a propensity to keep irrelevant things for decades just because her pride and joy sent it to her.

I cannot tell you how many times I have been preparing a case, secure in the knowledge that I had the document which would devastate the competition, only to realize that it had fatally entered my office, which I fondly refer to as "the dead zone." Once an original enters the door of my office, it is doomed to wander in limbo for all eternity—or, at least, until the exact moment when it is no longer relevant to anything on this earth.

It is for this exact reason that I tell my clients that I will not, under any circumstance, accept an original document from them. "Make a copy," I say. "The devil who loves to eat my originals seems to be allergic to copy toner."

Yet time and again I have stood in a courthouse hallway, ready to go to hearing, and have asked the client for the killer document only to be told "I thought I gave it to you."

(Of course, this is probably just the natural tendency of clients to lie to you when they realize that they did something stupid—like send the document to their Cousin Harry in Alaska who said he could analyze the thing and come up with devastating evidence, but who never received it because it was lost en route while being airlifted to Cousin Harry's remote tundra residence.)

I wish I could tell you the solution to this problem. I had it written down on a very important document but, well, you know...

The Lawyer's Weekend

I was sitting in my reading chair at 9 a.m. on a Saturday morning, reading about W.C. Fields. I was at the part where he was a juggler struggling through vaudeville and married with a child—a child, I might add, that he adored, contrary to his later image—when the phone rang.

"Mr. Bruce? We have a potential client on the line. He says he has a Federal case."

Of course I will talk to him. When you are a solo practitioner you can't readily turn down potential business because it happens to be the weekend.

Alas, the "Federal case" was actually a state misdemeanor and when I told him my very reasonable fees, I could hear him blanch on the other end of the line. Despite the fact that I'd just spent 30 minutes of my alleged weekend talking to him about the case, he gave me the classic "I'll call you later," line.

Ten minutes later I get another call, from the wife of a client whom I had managed to get out of custody the day before. He was in for alleged violence toward his girlfriend and had promised the judge he would leave the girlfriend alone and live with the wife if he was given an OR. The wife was calling me at 10 a.m. on a Saturday to tell me that the son of a misbegotten mother had gone straight back to his girlfriend, not even pausing at home to say hello to his loving wife.

Sigh.

The English have an expression: The Busman's Holiday. It comes from a comic story in which a bus driver goes on vacation in a bus and ends up driving the damned thing. So when you have to do your regular job on your time off, the English call it a busman's holiday.

In America we have something similar: The Lawyer's

Weekend. It's no weekend at all.

The Lawyer's Weekend. It is filled with anxiety, usually with a "quick" trip to the office that lasts about four to six hours, and calls and calls and calls.

It's filled with getting the mail at your office and finding out that the scum bucket on the other side of that civil case you're doing has filed a motion which needs to be answered by Monday morning.

It's usually crowded with the files you bring home "just to take a look" which end up piled up on the kitchen table after dinner. You pore through them while your family is sitting eating popcorn and watching a video in the front room.

The Lawyer's Weekend. There's even a joke that goes with it: Why do lawyers like Friday? Because that means it's only two more working days till Monday.

Why do we do this to ourselves? You go to a local county fair or a carnival or even just a damned farmer's market, and the whole time you have that criminal case appearance on Tuesday working in the back of your mind.

You sit drinking coffee with your spouse and she is talking about something the kid needs for school and the whole time you are nodding and saying "yes honey" and thinking that you need to do the research for that suppression motion in the possession for sales case which is set for trial next month.

You sit in church and the preacher is telling you about the loaves and fishes and it reminds you that you have to somehow make good case law appear out of nowhere in the family law case you have coming up next week.

The Lawyer's Weekend. If we could relax, we would. But if we could relax, we'd be accountants, not lawyers.

I wish I could tell you there's a solution. Or a cure. Or even a swift whack on the back of your head with a 2x4 which would allow you to forget for the space of Saturday and Sunday that you have clients who rely desperately on your acumen and tenacity.

I blame law school. When I was in law school I was

fresh out of journalism school, and I'd worked for a radio station. They let me have weekends. I would go home and not turn on the radio for two days so that my ears would stop ringing. And not once did I feel like I somehow was betraying my clients or losing ground on my opponents by not listening to the other DJ's shows.

In law school I discovered that when I was lolling the weekend drinking coffee and reading the Sunday paper, my fellow law students were encased in the school's library looking at the cases in the footnotes of the textbooks. And getting better grades than I.

(My revenge: Those people who worked so hard to get better grades went to work for big law firms who promptly expected them to continue that work ethic, making them show for 10 hours a day, six days a week, though they allowed them to work a paltry four hours on a Sunday).

Things did not change in the Real World. As a lawyer I know that while I sit in the sunny park eating a bologna sandwich, my evil opponent has locked himself in his office and is devising new ways to screw my poor client.

So even though I studiously avoid the office most weekends, the work follows me home. My spouse eyes me suspiciously when I start to twitch, knowing that I am thinking of my cases.

Then the phone rings again. And the Lawyer's Weekend continues.

What the Judge Thought

Good lord, am I going to have to put up with this guy again? The man can't lawyer his way out of a paper bag if the bailiff were to open the top and paint arrows for him. Now he's coming to me with a serious criminal case? Heaven help us all. Malpractice on a stick.

What's this? Is there something sarcastic in the way he calls me "your honor?" It's almost like he's questioning the validity of my black robe. I will smile back, of course—can't let my disdain for this clown dirty up the record. But I'm watching you, buckoo. Make one false move and it's handcuffs and a tiny cell for your three-piece butt.

Okay. Your motions are denied counsel. Denied. No, don't argue further. Denied. Yes, I've read the cases you cited. They all suck. Your moving papers suck. Your case sucks. Your client is so guilty that I'm going to have the bailiff sterilize the chair he's sitting in when I take the son of a bitch into custody. Yeah. Into custody. Let the guys in the tank teach him some manners.

Okay. Let's pick this jury quickly. What's that? You want to ask them about reasonable doubt? Why do you need to do that? We all know what reasonable doubt is. More or less. Okay, it's true that the jury instruction is somewhat blurry. That's the law, buddy. I'm not going to be the guy who changes it after eight hundred years. Neither are you. Move on, counsel.

Oh, for Pete's sake, we've been at this jury selection for half an hour. Why do we need to go through this tedium? I long for the days when we just took the first twelve fools...uh, jurors in from the street and started the trial. All this voir dire stuff makes me crazy. I wonder what's on TV tonight. I wonder if Margaret will be cooking pork chops tonight. Mmmm. Pork chops.

What's that? Oh, overruled. No, your objection is overruled, counsel. No, I don't think it's hearsay. Whatever the DA said, that's right. What did the DA say again? Sure. Spontaneous utterance. I don't care if the spontaneous utterance happened at the police station two days after the incident. It was spontaneous to the witness. Overruled. Move on, counsel.

Sigh. Okay, we can have a sidebar. Sure. What's bugging you, counsel? Priors? The witness has priors? Whose witness is this? The DA's? Then you can't use the priors. No, I don't care if they're drug dealing felonies. This case has nothing to do with drugs. Okay, it's another drug dealing case, so it does have something to do with drugs. I'm still not letting you use the priors as impeachment. No, I'm not. Sure. Object all you want. I'll have the clerk outline it in red and put little gold stars all around it. Move on, counsel.

The People rest. Thank God. Now we can go right to the conviction and—what's that? A motion to dismiss? And for what reason? That the only witness against your guy failed to recognize him? Didn't the cop recognize him as the guy he arrested for this deal? Sure he did. Good enough for me. Let's let the jury decide. Move on, counsel. Let's talk about jury instructions.

What? You're going to put your client on the stand? Do you think that's a good idea, considering how guilty he is? Okay. It's your funeral. Put the man on.

Priors? What's this about priors? He was previously arrested but not charged with possession of marijuana? Sure, Mr. Prosecutor, you can use that as impeachment. Counsel, you can object all you want, I've made my ruling. Explanation? Sure. This is a drug case and priors about drugs are relevant. The other witness? What other witness? Oh, that guy. I've made my ruling, counsel. Live with it. Move on.

Okay, let's finish this jury instruction thing quick as we can. Yes, we'll give all the reasonable doubt stuff.

See? I'm not such a bad guy, am I, counsel? Your special instruction? Give me the case law. Hmmm. Okay, the case seems to say what you say it says. So what? What do the People say?

Yeah, I agree. It's not really the same case. In that case it was cocaine. In this case it's meth. Completely different facts. Completely. No, I'm not going to give the special. No, you can cry all you want, counsel, but it's not gonna happen. Man up, for Pete's sake.

Okay. This DA is doing a pretty good job in his closing. Like the way he keeps saying the defendant is guilty. As he clearly is. What? You're objecting that the prosecutor brought up evidence which wasn't part of the trial? What was that? What his girlfriend said? What did she say in court? Oh, she never showed. Well, what the hell. Can't unring that bell. Mr. DA, please don't do that again. Okay? Sure. See? He said he won't do it again. No, I'm not going to give you a mistrial. No. No. No. Proceed, Mr. DA.

Okay, now this clown is giving his own summation. What an embarrassment. What law school did he go to—Robin Williams State? Good lord, that reasonable doubt thing is really a fetish of his, isn't it? Yes, Mr. DA, I am going to sustain that objection that he's saying "reasonable doubt" too much. Yes, I will personally admonish him in front of the jury. Jury, you are the sole judge of the facts and the law. Don't be mislead by this puppy.

Okay, now it's time to read the jury instructions to the jury. Hope I don't fall asleep again while reading them. Can't we get the clerk to do this? No? Sigh.

Okay, the jury's gone. Think I'll give the defense what for about what a lousy job he did on this trial and making him think twice before he sets foot in my courtroom again. Counsel, I—what's that, bailiff? The jury has a verdict? That was quick, but okay. I expected as much, as guilty as this guy is.

Ladies and gentlemen of the jury, do you have a verdict? Could you hand it to the clerk? The defendant will stand. That's right, you guilty piece of trash, stand. When I sentence you, you're going to go to state prison for so long your grandchildren will be serving your time.

What's that? Not guilty? Could you read that again, clerk? Are you sure? Sigh.

Well, ladies and gentlemen of the jury, thanks for your time. Now get out of my courtroom before I have the bailiff handcuff the lot of you.

What's that, Mr. DA? Yeah, I think you did a great job too. Guess we had some real losers in the panel. Mr. Defense? Sure. You're welcome. Uh...good job. Gulp.

Sigh. Wonder what Margaret is making for dessert tonight.

Thanks, Dean

My client and I sat in the courtroom as the jury filed back into the box. This moment is everything you've seen in any courtroom drama: The impassive faces of the jurors, the client tensed and shaking, the attorney's heart going *boom boom boom.* It had been a long time since I was this nervous about a verdict. I was sure my client was innocent. It had kept me sleepless the last three nights, going over every mistake I'd made in the trial.

I'd met her months before. Let's call her Mary, since calling her *the client* is rather cold. Mary was an attractive woman in her early 30s, a single mother with two kids, one of those bread and butter women who makes the world go round. She was accused of taking cash from her employer, but she told me that she was so stressed by her divorce and the thought that her ex-husband might take away her kids that she didn't notice that the money, for which she was responsible, was missing.

I like to think that, over the years, I've developed a sixth sense about clients. Many will tell you the truth, just as many will fudge it. Some will consider truth an option, but only as a last resort.

I listened to Mary as we met at a Jamba Juice all those months ago, I realized that she wasn't trying to play me, work me over, or even flirt with me. She was just telling the truth. She simply wasn't guilty.

Most Public Defenders will tell you that it's the innocent clients who cause you agony. The thought that one of *your* mistakes might send an innocent person to jail is enough to make you want to quit and become a plumber.

As 2003 had dawned and we waited for Mary's case to go to trial, I learned that one of my public defender mentors, Dean Allen, had died of cancer. Dean was my supervisor in the late 80s when I cut my teeth as a lawyer in Juvenile Court, working on everything from simple shoplifts to gang fights and robberies. Dean was a genial, scrawny man with a wicked but humane sense of humor. I had once done about 20 trials in a single month, including 4 in one day. When Dean gave me a day off the following month, I came into his office, concerned.

"Dean, why are you making me take the day off?"

"Because you earned it. You did more trials than anyone."

"Do I really need to take the day off?" I was a young lawyer and unaccustomed to the idea that lawyers were allowed to rest. Dean fixed me with his gray eyes and shook his head.

"Take the day off and that's an order," he said, "Or it'll go on your permanent record."

Years later when I was on the felony trial panel, I got out of court at 11 a.m. and decided to slip away to the gym for lunch. You usually hope, when you take such an unauthorized hour off, that no one will be the wiser. But as I spun on the stationary bikes, there was Dean coming up the stairs with his skinny white legs. He must've seen the guilty expression on my face. He smiled, put and finger to his lips and said, "I won't tell on you if you don't tell on me."

He taught me that it was okay to relax and be a human being even though you were a lawyer. But he'd also taught me that we work hard and fight for our clients because no one else will stand up for them. We present the human face of the client to the jury, he once told me. If we don't believe in justice, who will?

So now I sat as the clerk fiddled with the verdict form. Mary's hands were gripped tightly together in front of her. If the jury convicted her she'd lose her kids, her job, her life. I hoped the jury had seen what I saw in Mary, had seen the lies of the witness I suspected was the actual thief. But you never know. The DA's case was just good enough to make them forget the lies and convict. It happens every day in America.

The clerk read the interminable prelude to the verdict, my heart beating so hard it hurt. Then she read in a flat voice: Not Guilty.

Mary broke into hard tears, her body shaking. I found I was breathing again.

"Thank you, thank you," she said as she calmed down. This is what we do, I assured her, an unseen hand on my shoulder. I hope this will go on my permanent record, Dean. I couldn't have done it without you.

Short Stories
and Poems

At Family Court

A child is bouncing a ball
in front of the family law courthouse,
a boy, about six, his blond hair
cut like a mushroom around his head.
He throws the ball in the air, then tries
to catch it, running after
when it spills toward the women

sitting on a stone bench, talking
with stern expressions, hands
cutting the air in swift jabs;
the sun is out today, but they
don't notice it, can't allow themselves
to bask like children in its embrace.

On the elevator down to the plaza I saw
a pretty girl, face set like granite
tears staining her eyes. She clutched
papers from court and said nothing.
She was not the first person I'd seen
crying in the courthouse.

Now the child is tossing the ball
and hitting it with his hand.
He has found a playmate, a girl
with long blond hair, about six
years old. She tries to catch
the ball but he bats it away
and laughs. She finally sits down

and he takes the ball to a woman
who keeps it for a moment sternly
then laughs and throws it.
None of my clients showed today,
deciding the mental hospital
was more pleasant than court.

I talk to the coffee vendor
who popped a hamstring three weeks ago
pulling his coffee cart on a windy day.
It's his first day back. "I missed this,
God help me," he says, wry smile
stumbling across him. Now the child

takes the hand of another young woman
just out of the courthouse. The ball
is tucked under his arm. The blond girl
walks slightly ahead of them
scouting the street for stray cars.
The woman who had been crying
now buys coffee, her tears dry

but her face still in shock,
the cheeks still scored
by where the lines of tears
cut through like a wild stream
after a brief but brutal storm.

First Published in OC Lawyer, July 2002

Small Miracles

Why am I so queasy before a client is taken into custody? I envied other lawyers who took it with equanimity, who subscribed to the old expression: They go to jail, you go to lunch.

It's not as if I hadn't told Bremen over and over "If you pay no restitution, you're going to jail. Period."

"That won't be a problem," he had said. There was an oiliness in his manner that disconcerted me, but mine is not to judge. Clients like Bremen always thought they knew better than you did. And usually, they were terribly wrong. It's bitter satisfaction when your prediction of dire consequences comes true for a recalcitrant client.

Still, I hate to watch the bailiffs pull out the cuffs, hate to hear that annoying ratchet as the hasps are opened, hate that nasty click when they are fastened onto my client's wrists behind his back. It goes through me, it rattles my teeth, it makes me look over my shoulder for the rest of the day.

I climbed the stained gray concrete stairs leading up to Department 12, taking each step slowly. When I walked into the court, Bremen was sitting in the front row with his ghostly blonde wife, papers clutched in his hand. I nodded at him, then told the clerk I had arrived. She wrote my name down on the schedule. I noticed she had circled Bremen's case in red. The notation I saw—or thought I saw, for the clerk whisked it away pretty quickly—said "Possible custody. Alert Bailiff."

"How are we doing today?" I asked with false cheerfulness.

"Great," Bremen said, waving papers. "It's all here."

143

My heart lifted a little. Maybe this would be an easy day after all.

"So you paid some restitution?"

"I can."

I stopped. My heart failed to stick the landing and fell on its butt.

"You mean you did? Or you haven't yet?"

"Haven't yet, but I will, the whole $20,000."

I sighed.

"Come outside and let's talk," I said. He pulled his 300 pounds out of the chair and followed me out of the courtroom, his little wife trailing like a pilot fish.

We walked over to a bench in the corner of the hall. I looked around to make sure no one else was around—there are rules of confidentiality, after all—and sat down. I told myself not to get mad.

"Do you remember when we were in court last time?" I asked, trying to insert a patient tone into my voice without making it sound like I was talking to a five-year-old.

"Sure."

"Do you remember that Judge Delaney told me that she thought you were not going to pay any restitution and that she was giving you enough rope to prove that I was wrong about you and she was right?"

"Yeah."

"And do you remember when I told you that if you paid nothing, that she would put you in jail?"

"Yeah. And I can pay the whole thing."

"When? Today?"

"No, not today," he said, a bit annoyed. He waved the paper again. "But as soon as this goes through."

"What is that?"

"A refi on my house. I was working on it last time we were in court. I didn't want to tell you in case it fell through. But it's going to be approved tomorrow."

"A refi? You have a house? You didn't tell me you had a house." I wondered, briefly, if he had told the court of the house when asking for a public defender. Judges won't appoint us if the client has a home, on the theory that the defendant can get a loan on the house to hire a lawyer. To get a PD, Bremen would have had to sign, under penalty of perjury, a financial statement and statement of assets. I could see another charge in his future.

"...anyway, it's going to close tomorrow and I'll have all the money then." Bremen had been talking while I was thinking, not an unusual occurrence. I hoped I hadn't missed anything important.

"So tell me again why you couldn't pay the $8000 you said you had last time we were here. I have to know what to tell the judge."

"I needed it to leverage the refi. They needed to see some savings, and if I paid that into the restitution, I couldn't get the refi done."

I looked at him and he had that same air of outraged innocence I have seen on the faces of lying cops and used car salesmen.

"When are you going to get the money?"

"I can write you a check right now."

"You have the money right now?"

"No, but I can write a check and the court can hold it."

"The court's not going to do that. When will you have the money?"

"It's supposed to close tomorrow."

"Tomorrow is Saturday. Will they do business on a Saturday?"

"Sure. That's what they told me."

"Then write the check, but put the date on it when you think the money will be in the account. When will the money be available?" I was irked. I knew I was about to go into Judge Delaney's chambers and put on a minstrel show. I was sure what the outcome would be.

"Make sure you account for time for it to clear," his wife piped up.

"Okay, I'll make it out for today's date."

"Is the money there right now?" I said, impatience creeping into my voice.

"No."

"Then don't date it today. Then you've written a fraudulent check. You don't want more charges, do you?"

"When should I date it then?"

Suddenly we were in the middle of an Abbott and Costello routine:

"When will it be available?"

"Soon."

"How soon."

"A few days."

"Date it then."

"Date it today?"

"Not today, when it's available."

"When is that?"

"That's what I asked you."

"Today?"

"You said it won't be available today."

"It won't."

"Then don't date it today."

"Okay." He began to write today's date on the check. I looked at my watch, hoping the court would soon be closed for lunch. It was 9:30. I wondered what I could do to stall till noon. A fake heart attack? A sudden pager call from another court? Pushing my client down the stairs? That last option was the most attractive.

"Put June 28 on the check," his wife piped up. "That'll give us time." He added an "8" to the "2" he had already put on the check. He tore it out of the checkbook and gave it to me.

"Make sure they don't cash it today," he said. I pursed my lips and folded the check. He handed me the escrow papers and I glanced at them. They seemed to be authentic, but such things are easily forged.

"Okay, I'll do my best," I said. "But you know what I told you last time. No money, jail. If she takes you into custody, there's nothing I can do about it."

"If she takes me in, I won't be able to sign the refi papers tomorrow."

"I know. But I'm just telling you…"

"Okay," he said, sucking in his considerable gut. "We'll do what we've got to do, whatever that is."

"Don't disappear on me, either."

"What do you mean, 'disappear'?" His eyelids narrowed.

"Sometimes when I tell a client they might go into custody, they've been known to leave the courthouse. That's not a good idea. You do that, the judge will sentence you to state prison instead of local jail. You don't want that, I promise."

I looked him in the eye, trying to see if he was a runner. His brown eyes gleamed sharply. I hoped I wasn't giving him ideas.

"I'm not going to run," he said. For once, I believed him.

We went back into the courtroom, Bremen trailing me, the wife trailing the client. We looked like a sad circus parade—the ringmaster, the beast, the clown. The bailiff nodded at me and said "The DA's already back there on your case." I smiled tiredly and suppressed an old joke about *ex parte* communications. It didn't matter what the DA said. Judge Delancey would do whatever she wanted to do with Bremen.

Back in chambers the DA, an earnest young Latino fellow with glistening lips, was chomping on a cookie and drinking coffee. The judge was leaning back in her chair, hands behind her head, telling some story about her days as a prosecutor. She was a plump blonde in her early 50s, and you could tell she'd been a hellion in her youth. My supervisor, who had tried cases against her when they were both in their 20s, once told me that she was svelte and dangerous then.

"She once saw me in the hall when we were both misdemeanor deputies together," he said. "She said, 'you want to see my racing stripe?' Then she flipped her skirt up to show me her thong. I didn't know what to say. She laughed all the way to her office. I'm still not sure what

147

brought that on, as she was married at the time."

My own experiences with her had been mixed. She was rough, she was rude, and she often cut a lawyer off in mid-prevarication to say "That's bullshit and you know it is. What do you want? I'll tell you what I'm going to do no matter what you want."

I tried to look nonchalant as I sat in the chair

"What about Mr. Bremen?" she said, her wicked smile showing she'd already read the file. "Where's the restitution he promised?"

"Well, I know what you're going to do," I said, "so let me just be a public defender for a minute and whine."

She leaned back. "Whine away." She seemed very happy. She usually was, right before she took someone into custody.

I laid the paperwork on the desk. I explained about the refi and how he needed to have money in the bank to make it happen and how all restitution would be paid within a few days. The DA snorted at each twist and turn of the explanation. He didn't need to say anything.

"So he's given me nothing," she said, cutting to the point.

"Not yet." Better to just let it lay there. She picked up the escrow papers.

"So when is this refi going to happen?"

"He says tomorrow. He's written a check for when he thinks the funds will clear." I handed the court the check for $20,000.

"Is this an NSF check?" She took the check and sniffed at it melodramatically. "Yeah, smells like a bad check. What do you want me to do with this?"

"Hold it until he gets the refi done?" I didn't say this with much conviction.

She handed the check back to me.

"I'm not holding the check. I'll give him two weeks for the refi to go through and if it doesn't, he's in jail. Understand?"

For a moment, I didn't. To buy time I said, stupidly,

"You don't want to hold the check in the meantime?"

"I'm not a bank," she said, "And I don't keep bad checks. Tell your client that he has two weeks. Either full restitution is paid or he goes to jail. No home confinement. Understand?"

"Absolutely," I said, afraid to say anything else. Judge Delancey then leaned back in her chair and faced the side.

"I'm on this new diet and I've lost 50 pounds," she said. Now that she mentioned it, she did look a bit thinner. But perhaps that was just the haze of gratitude I was in for not forcing me to watch a client get cuffed.

"How'd you do that?" I asked.

"This high protein, low carb diet. It's something my doctor put me on. I feel pretty good. I want to lose a few more pounds then stop."

"That's great. Congratulations."

She eyed my little belly.

"Maybe you should think about it."

"Yeah, I've been trying to lose this tire for a few years, but nothing seems to work. I'm thinking about doing this eight minutes a day exercise and nutrition program I'm reading about right now."

"That won't work. I went to the gym for years. All it did was make me strong and fat. This is a good diet. You should try it."

"I'll look into it," I said, standing. I didn't want to risk saying something stupid to put her out of her mood.

"Okay, let's go out and do this," she said.

I came out and Bremen was gesturing at me. I waved him off as Judge Delancey walked through the side door.

"Remain seated and come to order," the bailiff barked.

"People v. Bremen," she said. Bremen stood and gestured at me again.

"Just follow my lead," I said. He looked at me doubtfully but said nothing.

"Mr. Bremen, I'm continuing your case for two weeks so you can come up with full restitution. You don't do it, you're going to jail. Is that clear?"

"Yes, your honor," he said.

"Good. Waive time?"

"Time is waived."

"Good. See you in two weeks." With that, she disappeared back into chambers.

We walked back into the hallway.

"So you know what you have to do," I said.

"Sure," the client said. "What if something happens?"

I stopped, queasy.

"What do you mean? I thought the refi was going to close tomorrow."

"What if it doesn't? What do we do then?"

"Listen, you heard the judge. If there's no restitution paid the next time we're here, you go in. I can't do anything else for you. I'm surprised about today, but small miracles still happen. God knows why."

I gave him my card.

"Call me if there's a problem. *Any* problem."

"Okay. I'm just not sure this is going to close by tomorrow."

"You told me twenty minutes ago it would. That's what I told the judge."

Bremen shrugged.

"You know how these things go."

Unfortunately, I know exactly how these things go. Suddenly I had a Public Defender epiphany: I was more worried about Bremen going into custody than he was. He came up with new excuses to keep himself out of custody, never expecting they would work. He was more surprised than I that he was still out.

"Just do your best," I said. My stomach hurt. I needed some coffee.

Motherhood

When I first met Barbara, she was in the tank, and her desperation was palpable.

"I have to get out," she said, "I have two kids who need me."

She was in for being under the influence of methamphetamine. The minimum on that is 90 days. She was not going to see her kids for a few months if she was found guilty.

"What about the charges?" I asked, naively.

"They're not true. I don't do drugs. I was at a party where other people were smoking dope and I must have had some kind of contact high."

The blood hadn't come back yet. Her story didn't sound quite right, but I was a young Public Defender and still wanted to believe my client's stories. I looked over the police report again and noticed that the cop had stopped her because she was alone in a high crime area. Otherwise, he would never have bothered her.

"Let me file a motion," I said. "I think I can get this thing dumped."

The gratitude in those luminous brown eyes was warming. She was pretty in a pixyish sort of way, small upturned nose, freckles, short brown hair. Petite. I felt my manhood stir a bit as she gazed at me with rescue in her eyes.

"I hope so, please do your best."

"I always do my best."

I took the file home. I went in on the weekend to do the research. Sure enough, the case law said that merely being in a high crime area was not enough to warrant a detention. All of the officer's observations had come after the

151

detention, so all of the evidence—including the blood results—was inadmissible. If a judge agreed with me, that is.

This is not always a given, even when you find a case dead on point. Some judges relish the challenge of finding exactly why a case with the same facts and the same issues as the one you cite should not have the same law applied to it. I wrote up the motion on Monday afternoon, and submitted it that day. Her case was coming up on Friday. Deputy DA Joyce Callin called me Wednesday.

"You've got to be kidding me," she said.

"In what way?"

"Come on. The results came back on the blood. This girl was doped up so much it's a wonder she's not dead. And you want to suppress evidence to get her out again?"

"So you're telling me the case law doesn't apply if your client is doped up."

"I'm saying that you're doing your client a disservice if you let her walk without getting her some help."

I knew I had a chance, then. The DA usually doesn't much care about the welfare of your client unless they think they might lose the case.

On Friday, Callin asked to talk about the case in chambers with the judge. The judge, Linda Morton, was an ex-DA who somehow had survived with some compassion intact. On the other hand, she rarely found for the defense on anything. Many a time I had to gently remind her (in the middle of a hearing) that she was not an advocate anymore, but a trier of fact. Once, at an arraignment, I had to stop her from examining my client about whether he committed the crime alleged before we could enter a not guilty plea.

"This girl is badly in need of a program," Callin said. This, from the Deputy DA who usually said that programs for hypes were a waste of time unless they were done in jail. "If we put her into a residential program, at least she'll have a chance to kick the habit. To let her out right now will only be allowing her to get deeper and deeper into her addiction. And she'll be back. "

Judge Morton had read the cases I'd cited. "I have no doubt she'd be back. The People are agreeing to allow your client to do a program instead of 90 days. What do you say, Mr. Roberts?"

"I say it's a damned good motion. But I'll ask my client."

When I came out into the courtroom they'd already brought my client up to the courtroom. She was sitting in her blue jail jumpsuit, which fit her snugly. She was looking anxious. From time to time she would look over at the front row, where sat two young girls, one about seven, the other about five. They were with an older woman. They were preternaturally quiet.

"What's going on?" she asked me.

"I filed the motion. The DA is worried about it. She'll let you do a drug program if you plead guilty today."

"Does that mean I'll get out?"

"Yes and no. It means you'll get out to go into the program. You won't be going home."

She started to cry.

"But my kids need me. I'm their only support. Their dad's disappeared a long time ago. I can't be away from them. It's going to kill me."

I let her go for a moment or two. You have to let them cry, no matter how much it annoys you.

"The blood came back positive for meth," I said. "Very, very positive. They say you were very intoxicated."

"That can't be true. I didn't do any meth. I only smoked a little dope."

"Maybe there was meth in the joint."

"I didn't think about that."

She began to cry again.

"Is this my only choice?"

"Of course not. We can still run the motion. If *this* judge doesn't hear it, we might even have a chance of winning."

Even though it was a good motion, I did not want to tell

153

my client to turn down the offer of a program on the off chance that some judge would actually follow the law.

"Okay," she said. There was a pause.

"Okay what?" I asked. I'd been burned before with clients seeming to agree to a deal, then telling the judge during the plea that they didn't really want it, the Public Defender had just assumed so.

"Okay, can we still do the motion?" She asked. She must have seen the surprise in my face. "Is that okay? Is there something wrong?"

"Not at all," I said. "I get points in my office for every motion I run. As long as you understand that if we lose, I can't get you the program."

She seemed to gather herself up. She put on a brave face. I felt the stirrings of admiration for her.

"I understand. I've got to do this for my kids."

When Judge Morton took the bench, she called Barbara's case. She looked down at me like a schoolmarm, fully expecting a plea.

"We're ready on the motion," I said.

Judge Morton pursed her lips. She looked over at Callin, who shook her head sadly, melodramatically. Then she said it:

"The People move to dismiss."

I couldn't believe I'd heard it. DA's hate to dismiss cases, but they hate even more to be beaten in a hearing. The motion was obviously better than I'd thought it was.

" Mr. Roberts, do you have an objection?"

Stumblingly, I agreed to dismiss the case.

"The defendant is released." With that, Linda Morton left the bench in a huff. She hated to see defendants go free, especially the guilty ones.

The little girls in the front row were ecstatic. They clapped and giggled and waved at Barbara. Barbara, who was again crying, waved back, mouthing "See you tonight." She turned to me. "Thank you," she whispered. I felt like a real lawyer. This, I told myself, was why I'd gone to law school.

A few weeks later, about ten at night, I had just come home and was pulling a TV dinner in the microwave. I was about to settle in for a tour around the cable channels, when my phone rang.

I have always been somewhat suspicious of calls after ten at night. The only cause for someone calling that late is an emergency, a death, or a request to borrow money.

"Hello, Jonathan?" said a vaguely familiar female voice on the other end of the line. The voice sounded tense, desperate.

"Yes," I said guardedly. I felt foolish for even giving this much information away.

"It's Barbara. Do you remember me?" The pixie face and lithe body flashed in my mind. I relaxed.

"Of course I do. How did you get my number?"

"You're listed in the book." I had not yet discovered that a Public Defender should never be listed in the telephone book.

"Of course I am," I said stupidly. "Is there something wrong?"

"Kind of," she said. I got the distinct impression that she was looking over her shoulder when she talked. "Can you come over here? To my house? Right now? I need your help."

"Is this something to do with court?"

"No. I just really need to see you."

I thought about it. It has never been a good idea to get involved in the personal life of a client. On the other hand, she was very pretty, and she wasn't my client anymore, thanks to the dismissal. I wasn't entangled with any woman at the moment, and so was especially vulnerable.

"Okay, tell me where you live."

There was a long pause. I could hear her breathing, but nothing else.

"Do I have to say it on the phone?"

"I won't know where you live otherwise. Just give me the address. I'll come over right away."

"But I don't know who's listening on the line."

"Does it matter? If it's the FBI, they already know your address anyway."

"Isn't there some other way you can come over here?"

"I've never been to your house before. Are you listed in the phone book?"

"No," she replied. There was another long pause. I was getting annoyed.

"Listen," I said petulantly, "if you don't want me to come over, I won't. But you called me, so it's your choice. Give me the address or hang up."

Reluctantly, she gave me the address. It was an apartment house about ten minutes from where I was living. I put on some clothes and drove over, making sure to eat my TV dinner quickly before I left.

The apartment was on the edge of what we called "ghost town"—the area where the marginal people lived. I'm sure I passed a drug dealer on the corner, who eyed me as a prospective customer. Any white guy in a relatively recent model car was probably looking for something illegal. The buildings had a sag and grit to them. I found the apartment address: A brown place with a sloped roof. The door on her apartment was peeling, the number barely visible. I knocked.

I waited. There was no stirring in the apartment, but I could see the peephole darken for a moment a few seconds after I rang the bell. She'd seen me, but she wasn't about to open the door.

"Barbara?" I asked. "You called me. I came over. Where are you?"

No answer. I thought I heard a faint rustle in the apartment, but it might have been the wind on the landing.

"Barbara?" I said again, ringing the doorbell. "It's Jonathan. If you don't answer the door in one minute, I'm going to leave."

I heard the ethereal ring of a lock being disengaged. Then the faint complaint of a door being opened an inch. One of her brown eyes examined me carefully.

"Is that you, really?"

"Yes," I said. I had come expecting some show of gratitude for what I had done for her—say, a nice dinner, some light conversation, some perfectly ethical sex. She wasn't my client anymore, and I was allowed. It happens in the movies all the time. But her caution was dampening my ardor.

She pulled the door back quickly and pulled me by the arm. I went into the apartment and she shut the door fast.

"They're out there, I know they are."

"Who is that?"

"The people spying on me."

"Who is that?"

"I think the manager's in on it. I think that the lady next door is in on it. There's others I don't recognize."

She was dressed in a t-shirt and jeans. The jeans fit tight on her slim body and I allowed myself to feel amorous once again. I was young. I hadn't had a woman for months. And if she seemed a little desperate, well, we'd deal with whatever was bugging her and then get down to business.

She walked into the living room, sparse with a shabby green couch and some ten dollar paintings on the walls. A television sat on an old stand, and the rabbit ears stuck out at an odd angle. She didn't sit down.

"I know they're listening, so I don't want to say much," she said.

"Listening?"

She put her finger to her lips, then gestured for me to follow her. She walked into the hallway again and opened, carefully so that it made almost no noise, a cupboard. There were towels and sheets stacked in the cupboard. She pulled one towel aside and pointed at something that looked like a bracket holding the shelf in place.

"What's that?" She said.

"Looks like a bracket to me," I said.

"What's a bracket?"

I explained the concept to her, though I've never been

157

much of a carpenter.

"It looks to me," she whispered, "like a bugging device. I know they're listening in on me. I think they're trying to find out something."

"Why would they be spying on you?" I asked, not bothering to ask who *they* were.

"I don't know," she said, beginning to cry. "But I've noticed the manager looking at me funny lately, and I've noticed that every time I come home the next door neighbor happens to be on the porch. And I hear weird things at night, like voices talking. I think they've bugged my phone. I think they're taking movies of me as I go in and out. For all I know there are cameras all over this apartment. The manager has a key and can get in anytime he wants..."

She went on like this for ten minutes. I kept trying to take her by the arm and sit her down on the couch, but she shook me off.

"Where are your kids tonight?" I asked.

Her eyes flashed suddenly. She reappraised me.

"Why do you want to know?"

"I just wondered. I remember them from court."

"They're with a friend. They're okay. I didn't want them here while I was being spied on. It's not safe. God knows what they'll do to me. I don't want them here for that..."

And off she went again.

"Come, sit on the couch," I said, taking her slim waist in my arm. I tried to steer her back to the living room, but her body stiffened.

"I don't want to go in there. Let's just stay here."

"In the hallway?"

"For now. It's not safe."

"What is going to happen to us if we go into the living room?"

"That's too near the window."

"Well, what about the bedroom?" Why not go for broke?

"No, I'm sure that they've bugged the bedroom, too."

I kept trying to put my arm around her shoulders, her waist, anything that would allow me to steer her to a sitting position. Each time she would let me walk her a few steps, then she would suddenly turn away and go back into the hall.

"Why are they doing this to me?" She said. She was almost in tears.

"I'm not sure who's doing anything to you, Barbara."

"You don't know, you just don't know."

After an hour and a half of this, even my young man's hope of intimacy had been beaten down, and I'd had enough.

"Listen," I said finally, "I'll go outside and check if it's safe. If it is, you can come with me and we'll go somewhere else where they're not looking at you, okay?"

"You're going to put me into a hospital, aren't you?"

Surprisingly, the thought hadn't crossed my mind. And, of course, there was no good answer to this question.

"I have to go," I said. "I have to work in the morning. You can either come with me back to my apartment, or you can stay here. You choose."

In response, she went into the hallway and stared again at the brackets. I let myself out.

Later that night, about 2 a.m. the phone rang again. I drowsed out of a hard sleep and answered it without thinking.

"Jonathan?" It was Barbara.

"What is it?" I asked.

"I need you to come over here. I can't tell you why on the phone."

I almost said, *unless you're naked and ready for me, I'm not going anywhere.* But even when groggy I had some professional reserve.

"I can't do that," I said. "Go to bed and call the police in the morning."

I hung up as she continued to talk. I put my answering machine on and went back to bed. The phone rang four

159

more times that night, each time her desperate voice scraping on the machine with the same thing: *Jonathan, you've got to come over here. It's important. I can't tell you why on the phone. Please, you're my only hope. I don't know who else to call. Please come over. Please please please please please....*

Two days later I was in the custody tank talking to a client on her third DUI. Suddenly, I heard a voice.

"Jonathan, you've got to help me."

I looked over. Barbara was back in custody.

"What are you doing in there?" I asked before I could stop myself.

"They say I was under the influence. But I don't do drugs, you know that. You've got to help me. My kids need me."

I looked at the calendar which lists all cases and the deputy handling each. Her name was across from another lawyer's. I breathed easier.

"Mr. Chavez will be helping you today, Ma'am," I said politely.

"It's got to be you, Jonathan, you're the only one who can help me."

I nodded, then turned my back to her. I continued to fill out the plea form for the lady with the DUI. That afternoon, I called Pac Bell and got an unlisted number.

Ethics

She was beautiful but he couldn't touch her. Well, he *could* touch her, but then he'd lose his bar card. She was his client.

And today she'd worn a tight, tight silk synthetic dress that hugged her thighs and showed him crevices no sane man should see in daylight. She leaned toward him and said, almost in a whisper, "I can't go to jail."

He looked at her. As she leaned toward him, he could see her two plump breasts, barely nestled inside her dress. Little pink nipple played hide and seek with the folds of the fabric. She'd neglected to wear a bra. Of course she had.

His first inclination was to reach in and take hold of one of those beauties, caress it, finger the hint of nipple and say to her, "Of course you're not going to jail, my dear. How could we think of putting something as delicious as you into such a nasty place as the Orange County Jail?" He swallowed hard and brought his gaze up to her eyes. Big mistake. Blue and clear and clearly seeing that he was clearly seeing her.

He wanted to take her into a dark corner and commit acts of unethical behavior with her. Instead he tried to put on his best lawyer voice and said "Well, Miss Connors, I'm going to do my best. The law kind of limits what I can do on a suspended license charge." Suspended license? What cop in his right mind would give a piece of ass like this a suspended license ticket? Probably a woman cop.

"But I just can't see myself in jail," she said. He tried to envision her in a baggy orange jumpsuit but he kept looking at the curve of the silk dress from her waist toward her legs. This wasn't doing him any good. It wasn't doing her any good, either. She was romancing the wrong stone here. He was just a PD, her court appointed lawyer. He had no power. She might as well be seducing the janitor.

"Well maybe I can convince the DA to give you a driving without a license charge," he said, feeling like a goddamned teenager. "That wouldn't carry a mandatory jail sentence."

"That would be great," she said, accidentally rubbing against him. He allowed himself the image for a moment: Her case over, they meet by chance in a bar. She gets drunk (why do all his fantasies involve the woman getting drunk first? Some serious self esteem issues there, boy). Then she goes down on him on the way home and they pull over and...

"Hey, Carter," the DA broke his reverie. It was Christos, the Greek child with the shiny lip gloss. "What are we gonna do with suspended license girl?"

"I was thinking--"

"No 12500." That was the driving without a license charge.

"Why not?"

"This is her second one. The first happened the day before. She's popped the day before and she drives again."

"Maybe she didn't believe the first cop."

"It's a loser. I'll give her the minimum, five days in jail."

"She doesn't want to do jail time."

"No one does. But that's the minimum."

"Have a heart, Christos. I got a big calendar today and need to clear this one."

"Yeah, I saw her. I wouldn't mind clearing her either."

Carter blushed, surprised at himself. Hey, he was a healthy young man. Why couldn't he notice that his client had a body that put a Corvette to shame? He was about to make a salty comment to recover his manhood, when he noticed Christos was gone.

He walked over to her and squatted beside her. She sat in the courtroom, girlfriend by her side. The girlfriend wasn't bad, either.

Jesus, what was wrong with him? This was misdemeanor court, not a strip joint. Put it back in your pants, buddy.

"I'm wearing the DA down," he told her. "But it might take some time. Do you want to come back in a few weeks?"

"Will it help?"

"Couldn't hurt. He's offering the minimum now."

"What's that?"

"Three hundred dollar fine and five days."

"Five days of what?"

"What do you think?"

"I can't do jail time." She inclined her head so that it touched his. He could smell some strange pungent perfume, an elixir of roses and violets and something demonic. "I know you can get this for me."

"Sure I can. But it's gonna take time."

She sighed and leaned her head back.

"Okay. Do I have time to smoke a cigarette?"

"Yeah, go ahead."

She got up and walked out. The dress clung to her ass and revealed a nice little shelf above the cheeks. It was small and round like a cup holder, and he got a bizarre vision of doing her from behind and setting a beer in that little cleft.

He felt his hand tremble. He needed to get her off his calendar before he did something stupid. One more hour with her and his hands wouldn't be his own. He had a terrible vision of Judge Martinez on the bench, staring down at him in her schoolmarm fashion, while he groped Connors in the aisle. He shook his head. Had to get her out of here fast.

Christos was waiting for him, his puppet's face in a smile.

"I guess you're a hell of a lawyer," he said. "I'm gonna give you the 12500 on your girl."

"Really? You're a star, Christos." The DA was smiling. He couldn't figure out why, but he never trusted a prosecutor who smiled when he gave you a good deal.

Connors was delighted, gave him a big, sloppy hug, her plump breasts brushing his chest. He felt himself becoming aroused and removed himself from her before she could tell. She gave him that secretive smile beautiful women give to let you know that they know.

The plea went quickly. She agreed to pay a $50 fine and get her license. He watched her walk out of court. She walked slowly, to give him something to dream on later.

Two minutes after she left, the bailiff handed Carter her minute order. "She might need this," he winked at Carter. His heart beating hard, Carter dashed out the courtroom, delighted to have one more chance to see her, maybe to say "Now that you're not a client anymore..."

He stopped dead when he turned the corner outside the courtroom. There she was, with her blonde friend. And there was Christos, the Greek dog, chatting at both of them, giving Connors a slip of paper with his telephone number on it, his puppet face and glistening lips already moving as if he had her nipple between his perfect white teeth.

The Evil Twin Defense

I stood near the orange bars with the man's file, and watched as he sauntered over to me. He was tall, with bright red hair which almost matched the color of the bars. His jail jumpsuit fit him poorly, only coming down to an inch above his ankles. He had a hawk nose and a tall forehead. What concerned me were his eyes: They were the kind of luminescent black you'd see at the edge of darkness around a wilderness campfire. They glowed with equal parts anger, defiance and hope, on the wrong side of sane by an inch. They bored into me as he loped through the wire mesh door and into the interview area.

The interview area of the North Court jail was actually just a cleared concrete floor where the lawyers could talk to the clients away from the cells full of other inmates. On a busy day, like this one, the lawyers lined the outside of the cage, standing with their files open and papers flopped over the manila folders. The clients leaned against the bars, looking intently at the files, as if trying to read tea leaves. My client, however, did not so much as glance at his file.

I could smell him before he stopped—a smell like unwashed clothes, even though he had on a clean jail suit. I introduced myself as his Public Defender and he nodded, saying nothing.

"Today is a day for pretrial," I said, going into my normal litany. "This is a day for me to talk to the judge and the prosecutor on your behalf to see what would happen if you decided to plead guilty."

"I'm not pleading," he said.

"Well, let me tell you what the offer is—"

"I'm not pleading. Not to anything. I'm not guilty. I'm an innocent man, and I'm going to trial to prove it."

I paused. This was a complication I didn't need.

"Well, let's talk about the case," I said. "They seem to have photos and a video of you, taken by the bank, as you went in and tried to withdraw money from your father's account..."

"Do you have the photos?"

"Not yet."

"Check the photos. I'll bet they're not me."

I looked at him. The man resembled nothing so much as a gooney bird, with his long limbs and beaked nose. If I could get the bank photos, there would be no mistaking him.

"If I get the photos and it's you, would you change your mind?"

"I won't have to change my mind because it's not me and I'm not guilty."

He watched me intently as he said this. Though I was young, I had learned early that there were some clients you couldn't argue with.

"Okay," I said, "I'll ask the DA to get the photos for us. I'll set another pretrial a week from now, before the trial date. Then we can look at the photos together."

"Good," he said, mollified. "You'll see. You have an innocent client."

"Great," I said, with only a trace of facetiousness, "that would be a welcome change."

Up in court I told Margaret Collins, the deputy DA on this case, that we needed the photos for another pretrial next week. She gave me a sidelong glance, but wrote in her file to have the photos by next week.

"Do you think he'll plead if I get the pictures?" She asked. She didn't really want to do this trial. Family squabbles tended to get unnecessarily messy in the courtroom.

"I'd have to see the pictures first," I said noncommittally.

"I've seen them," she said. "And I don't think there's much doubt it's your client."

"If you've seen them, then you have an obligation to show them to me, don't you?" I said, trying to strike the balance between friendly suggestion and professional warning. The DA is required to show us all the evidence they have against our clients, whether they intend to use it or not. The younger DA's on the misdemeanor panel resented this. It took all the sport out of the trial. Margaret made a little sour face at me.

"Okay," she said, "I'll get the pictures. You can see for yourself."

A week later Margaret sat in the courtroom caressing a folder with photos and looking like she'd just dipped her fingers in cream.

"I've got them," she said, "now it's your turn to convince your client that it's time to stop playing games and plead out."

"I'll show the photos to Mr. Farmer and see what he says." She glared at me, and gave a hiss of exasperation. I walked over to where my client was sitting, handcuffed, in the jury box. The judge had brought up all of our pretrial clients, hoping to get them done quicker if she eliminated the long trek between courtroom and tank. And, for that matter, side trips by the lawyers from the courtroom to the tank and then the lunch wagon for a 20 minute cup of coffee.

I showed Farmer the photos. There he was, in grainy black and white, all six foot something of him, leaning on the bank counter, holding a passbook. In the photo he wore a mesh t-shirt and parachute pants. His bald head and beaked nose shone in the bank's soft fluorescent. No one in their right mind would believe it was anyone other than him.

"That's not me," he said flatly. The courtroom was noisy, and I was half deaf. I leaned back in and cocked my ear toward him.

"I'm sorry, I'm not sure I heard you."

"That's not me," he said again. "Look, that guy is bald. I have hair. And that guy is shorter than I am. That's not me. I'm innocent."

I looked again at the photo, trying to see what he had seen.

"I have to tell you," I said carefully, "it looks an awful lot like you."

"Look how grainy and fuzzy it is. How can you say it's me?"

The photo *was* a bit grainy and fuzzy. But I was coming to realize that my client was as well.

"If it's not you," I said slowly, "then who is it?"

I asked this rhetorically. So when the answer came, it was an unwelcome surprise.

"That's Tom Bottoms."

"Okay. Who's Tom Bottoms?"

"He's a friend of the family. We've known him for years. He looks just like me. He's always getting me in trouble. He's a real crook, takes drugs, steals from everyone. A liar. It's been a family joke for years that he's my evil twin."

There it was: The evil twin defense. The staple of many a 30s movie, the standing joke among criminal law attorneys. When in doubt, use the evil twin defense. That *always* gets 'em.

The client had even used the words himself. I was not happy. The DA was going to be less so. The judge least of all.

"Are you sure you don't just want to take the 90 days the judge is offering right now? After trial it could be a year. Or worse, the D.A. could re-file this as a felony. It was over $15,000. It's only in misdemeanor land because it's a family matter."

"I'm sure. You've got an innocent client." He said this last so intently that I could feel his hot, baloney-scented breath on my neck as he leaned down toward me. "I'm innocent," he said again. "You're representing an innocent man."

I wondered if he believed that by repeating the word "innocent" it would somehow reverberate throughout the cosmos and create a harmonic convergence between himself and the prosecutor to get the case dismissed. I looked over at Margaret, who was scowling like a Roman. She must've missed the harmonic convergence.

"I'll do my best," I said. This is the phrase I use when I know that I am in trouble.

The next day I was sitting at my desk at 4:30 trying to finish my files so that I could get out by five. I was hoping to get to the gym to work out some stress. Then the phone rang.

I hesitated before I picked it up. It's never a good sign when the phone rings at 4:30 in the afternoon. No one rational is still working on anything at that time, especially in the Misdemeanor world. But my sense of duty, which gets me into more trouble than I care to think about, prevailed. I answered the phone.

"Mr. Farmer is calling," the secretary on the other end said, "should we accept the charges?" Our clients in custody have to call us collect.

"Go ahead." I waited while the secretary clicked over the line.

"It's me." The voice said.

"What can I help you with, Mr. Farmer?"

"I was just thinking," he said. It's always dangerous for a client to try thinking, especially while in custody. For many of them unfamiliar with the process, the attempt to contemplate anything in such a setting inevitably leads to mischief.

"If you're wondering," I said, "I have an investigator trying to find Tom Bottoms. I haven't heard anything back on that, yet."

"I'm thinking about my father. I think he's in on this with Tom Bottoms."

"Your father is conspiring with the evil twin to keep you in jail? And why is that?" I hoped I didn't sound too incredulous, but I'm only human.

"I think my father's been cashing my royalty checks. I think he's been keeping the money in the bank account they say I was trying to get into. I think he wants to keep the money, which is hundreds of thousands of dollars, and if he knows I'm in custody, he can keep the money for himself."

"Slow down, Mr. Farmer. Your father is cashing royalty checks? From what? An oil well?"

"I'm a songwriter. I wrote a lot of hits. You ask Linda

Ronstadt. You ask Elton John. And Olivia Newton John. They've recorded a lot of my songs. They know me personally. They'll come into court and say so."

"I'm sure they will," I said, noncommittally.

"Of course they will. And if they don't you can subpoena them into court. Didn't you tell me we could subpoena anyone we needed into court?"

"I did say that, but I was thinking about people who might be alibi defense witnesses."

"Call Linda Ronstadt. She knows me really well. Subpoena her, if you have to."

"Mr. Farmer, I'm not going to subpoena Linda Ronstadt."

There was silence on the other end. I should have known better than to be blunt.

"Then you're in on it, too."

"Mr. Farmer, I'm not in on anything. I'm working late on a Friday afternoon and I'm trying to get all of my cases handled for all of my clients. If I asked the investigator to subpoena Linda Ronstadt, they'd laugh me out of the office. And if I insisted, the office would likely get sued by Linda Ronstadt's attorneys."

"I'm an innocent man," he said. "And I need to show why my dad is conspiring against me."

The word a public defender dreads most to hear from his client is the "c" word. You know, then, that your client is sailing in another dimension, one you can only guess at. I tried to think of something to say to mollify him.

"Look, I'll look into getting someone to talk to Linda Ronstadt's people."

"Not her people, Linda Ronstadt."

"I'll do my best," I said. "Meanwhile, try to be calm. We have trial on Tuesday and I want you to be in good shape for that."

There was a long silence on the other end. I could tell he was trying to decide whether to keep me or to ask the judge for a new lawyer. Either way, I would still be on the case—if he asked for a new lawyer, we'd have to have a full hearing in a closed courtroom, and I would have to tell the judge every little thing I'd done on the case. Then the judge would tell the client, nicely, that I'd done about as much as a lawyer can do, and deny the motion. In the end I'd still be on the case with a disgruntled client who would mutter throughout the trial. The motion is a waste of time and gives the judge too much insight into your client. They're hearings I try to avoid.

"I'm working on your file right now," I lied blithely, "and I'm working on a defense. If we find Tom Bottoms, seems to me that's enough for reasonable doubt. If we try to get other issues into the case, the judge might blow up and punish you harshly."

"I'm already in jail. What can she do worse?"

Good question, one I hadn't expected from a client using the "c" word.

"I don't want to find out. Let's just focus on the trial Tuesday and work on what we can do to win, okay?"

"Okay," he said. He sounded stronger. "Thanks."

"Don't mention it. Just doing my job."

A few days later Marty Watkins, one of the public defender investigators, wandered into my office. Marty was an older investigator who'd come to our office after retiring from the New York police. He'd done twenty years with the NYPD, and was on his second decade with us.

"I got this investigation request," he said, his voice tainted with disbelief. He held my request on Farmer. "At first I thought this was a joke. Thought you were trying to play a prank on one of my younger investigators. But I know you wouldn't do that. What gives?"

I shrugged. Marty was struggling not to show disdain.

"The client insists that this is true," I said. "I think we have an obligation to check it out."

"Okay," Marty said, and he sat in my chair. "I talked to the father on this case. He says his son's nuts. Sad case. Nice guy, the dad. Get your client to plead."

With that he stood up and walked out. *Get your client to plead.* In some cases, easier said than done.

On the day of trial the judge brought up Mr. Farmer one more time. I had talked to her about the case in chambers and she, to my surprise, had offered to let him out today if he would plead. This offer of "Credit Time Served" was the holy grail for many of my clients, and often as mythical. But Farmer's case was just wacky enough that everyone wanted to avoid trying it.

When my client arrived in the courtroom, his pale orange jumpsuit sagging, he nodded at me as if we were old friends. I walked over to him and talked in a low tone.

"The judge has offered to let you out today if you plead guilty." I left it at that.

"What does that mean?" He said. I allowed myself some hope. Since he didn't reject the offer outright, there might be a chance he would see reason.

"It means that if you plead guilty today, the judge will give you credit for the time you've been in custody and put you on informal probation."

"I don't want no probation officer."

"You won't get one. Informal means you don't report. You just have to stay out of trouble for the next three years."

He was quiet for a minute. I could tell he was thinking about it. Then I made a fatal error. I kept talking.

"We've tried to find Tom Bottoms and we can't," I said. "Your father doesn't think he exists."

This didn't have the effect I had hoped it would. The man straightened up. His eyes grew narrow. His fists clenched into a very painful-looking ball. I would not have been surprised to see blood trickling from where his fingernails dug into his palms. His mouth tightened and I could see his jaw muscles working.

"I'm not guilty," he said. "I'm innocent. My dad knows this. He and Tom Bottoms are in on this together. I want a trial."

"After trial you might get up to a year."

"I want a trial. I'm innocent."

"You'll be in custody during the trial."

"That's okay. I'm willing to do that to prove my innocence."

"If we don't find Tom Bottoms, you're going to have to testify."

I suppose I thought this would terrify him, would convince him to take the easy way out. But the man smiled, and a strange illumination came to his face.

"I *want* to testify," he said. "I live for the day I can tell my story to the jury."

I looked deeply at him and realized that there was no chance now that he would *ever* plead. This was no longer a trial: It was going to be therapy. And high drama. And vindication. Pleading would end the opera before the first aria.

I had learned as a public defender that if you keep pushing a client who doesn't want to plead, he will begin to wonder whose side you're on. There's a term for PD's who plead out all of their clients: A dump truck. I didn't want to have that reputation in the jails.

Mr. Farmer looked at me with the same expression of disdain that Marty had tried to suppress the week before.

"If you're not willing to do the trial," he said, "maybe I should do it myself."

My belly turned to ice at the thought. A man has a right to represent himself. But then, a man has a right to take a two by four and slam it into his head repeatedly. In either case, it's never a very good idea. And I didn't want to have my client tell the court he wanted to represent himself because his public defender didn't want to try the case. Reputations are funny things. Once it gets out that you're afraid to try a case, the justice system begins to treat you like a second class lawyer. The DA's who think you're afraid of trial give your client lousy offers. The judges treat you like a special education child. And the public defender's office finds a nice, safe place to park you so that you don't have to be put to the agonies of trial—like doing probation violation hearings.

"I'm on your side, big guy," I said with false familiarity. "If you want a trial, I'm going to make sure you have the best chance you can have. I just want to make sure you know what you're up against before we do this. That's part of my job."

He nodded. He wasn't taken in by the "big guy" routine, but he at least was satisfied. I relaxed a little. After all, the worst that could happen to Mr. Farmer was a year in custody. That wouldn't be so bad, would it?

The judge took the bench. She shuffled her files like playing cards. Finally, she found ours.

"Darren Farmer."

"Thank you, your honor. We're ready on that."

There was a stifling pause. The judge looked at me with a mix of surprise and anger. Her lower lip tightened.

"You're ready for what, counsel?"

"Trial," I said, simply. I could hear Margaret hiss behind me. I didn't dare look over at her. I could hear her flopping her files loudly.

"Counsel, did you explain to your client that I'm making a CTS offer?"

"Of course, your honor."

"And that means that he gets out tonight?"

"Yes, your honor."

"And he still wants to go to trial?"

"I'm an innocent man," my client said, a wheedling tone in his voice. The judge regarded him sharply.

"I can't give you a better offer than CTS," she said.

"I'm innocent, your honor."

"I think you're being foolish, Mr. Farmer. At the end of trial, I could give you a year in jail, has your lawyer told you that?"

"Yes he has. He's told me everything. He's done his job. I want a trial. I want a chance to tell the jury my story."

She stared at him a long minute. She'd been on the bench for years and had been a public defender herself, once. I think she recognized the illumination in the client's face, that expression of the clients we call *kamikazes*. For a brief second, she gave me an understanding and sympathetic glance.

"All right. Madame clerk, call up a panel."

In our office we had a closet full of civilian clothes for in-custody clients to wear at jury trial. (It's unseemly to have your client go through trial in an ill-fitting orange jumpsuit with "Orange County Jail" stenciled all over it.) By some miracle, I found a pair of pants long enough to fit him, and a baggy shirt. I went down to the tank, gave the clothes to the sheriff's deputy in charge with instructions that my client dress out in them before we returned to court that afternoon.

At 12:45, as I was looking over the case, I got a phone call from the deputy.

"Your client says he won't put on these clothes."

"Excuse me?"

"Your client says these clothes aren't good enough for him and he won't dress in them. I suggest you come down and talk to him."

I left his file open on my desk and once again descended to the tank. As I entered the attorney area, he was already standing there, swaying back and forth like an elephant in the zoo.

"Mr. Farmer—"

"I'm not going to wear those clothes. They make me look like a clown."

"I'm sorry, that's all I could find."

"You're in on this, aren't you?"

"In on—no, I'm not. I'm trying to help you. But you're a very tall man. Do you agree that you're taller than the average client?"

He looked around at the sea of heads, all nodding and talking to their attorneys. He was a head taller than any of them. He bowed his head.

"So what I found is the best I could find. Maybe I could find another shirt, but the pants are the only ones we have in your size. You don't want to walk in there wearing flood pants, do you?"

He chuckled at this. My guess is, at his size, he'd often had to wear pants whose hem didn't quite reach his ankle.

"If I found another shirt, would that help?"

"Yeah. A blue one. Blue is a lucky color for me."

"I'll look," I said. Back upstairs, I sorted through the closet and found, after handling too many shirts, a pale blue nylon number that would not have been out of place on the set of *Saturday Night Fever*. It was the only blue one we had. I had also found a white shirt that was bland but respectable, so I took them both. If he had a choice, he'd be much happier. I gave the shirts to the deputy.

His expression was completely bland as he searched the pockets and seams for contraband. Then he clicked on the intercom.

"I have two shirts for the fashion model's approval," he said, flipping me a quick sidelong glance. I smiled and left. At least the deputies understood.

When my client appeared in the courtroom that afternoon, he was wearing the polyester shirt, buttoned all the way up. He was smiling and even joked with me a little that he thought he looked quite rakish.

My client was the only person in the courtroom happy to be there. The judge was grumpy to have to start a trial on a Thursday, in the afternoon, on such a simple matter. The jury was equally angry at the prospect of sitting on a case today, Monday and Tuesday. Needless to say, Margaret was calling me "Counsel" in a clipped tone and only spoke to me when she absolutely had to.

"This is going to be fun," my client said.

During voir dire he continually whispered in my ear during the DA's questioning. He said aloud several times, "that's not true" when she talked to the jurors about what the law said about theft and reasonable doubt, and he was admonished by the judge. When I had questioned the jurors before the DA, he had sat silent as a cat.

He pored over the jury panel carefully.

"I don't like the lady in the blue dress," he said. "She's been giving me the evil eye." This lady was the one juror who had responded well to my questions, even saying that sometimes family squabbles should not be brought to criminal court. But to make him happy, I took a peremptory challenge and kicked her off the jury.

This was a mistake. Farmer perceived that he had the power to say *yea or nay* to up to ten people on the panel, and he was determined to use every one of them. So my engineer who might have forced the DA to an excruciating proof of the facts? Gone because he had a beard, and beards are a sign of dishonesty. My homemaker with a nephew with mental illness (which would make her sympathetic to my client)? Gone because she was too fat and fat people have something to prove to the world. My college student who had a run-in with the law and was therefore somewhat suspicious of the whole process (and who, to my amazement, the DA left on the panel?) Gone because he was too young to understand what my client had been through in Vietnam.

We were left with an aged, scowling, Mount Rushmore of a jury in whose eyes I saw a coldness that made me shudder. These days, of course, when the client wants me to kick a juror, I pat the client on the back, make a show of listening to comments, then pick the jury I want. After all, you get a lawyer in a criminal case to make such decisions for you.

During the DA's opening Farmer kept whispering loudly "she's lying" and "that's not true." Finally, the judge called me up to the bench.

"If your client continues to make such comments," she said, "I'll remove him from the courtroom."

"Your honor, he's just a little excited."

"I've noticed," she said dryly. "But in my courtroom I don't allow such outbursts. Tell him to keep quiet."

I told him this and could see him about to explode, so I added: "She means it. You'll be gone very quick, then we'll do the trial without you." This calmed him quickly. He wanted to watch the trial at all costs, even if it meant keeping quiet. He shook his head, leaned back in his chair, and closed his eyes

When I gave a short opening, asking the jury only to examine the evidence carefully, I could feel him scowling behind me. I sat down and he leaned over to me.

"Why didn't you tell them that my father was lying so that he could steal my royalty money? Why didn't you tell them about Tom Bottoms?" He whispered right into my face. I wondered whether the jail ever fed my clients anything else but baloney.

"I want those things to be a surprise," I said. He smiled and sat back in his chair. I have never understood why clients are much happier and more comfortable if they think you're about to pull magic tricks during the trial.

The first witness was the bank teller. She was a thin, blonde girl, no more than nineteen years old. She had a nice, round face and was rather timid on the stand. In other words, she was eminently credible.

"Do you see the man who tried to use Mr. Farmer's savings account passbook?" the D.A. asked. To help the witness, Margaret turned and angled her body toward my client. The clerk stared at the redheaded bird sitting next to me and nodded. There was a pause while Margaret waited.

"Where is the man you saw?" she said, with only a little exasperation.

"Right there. Next to the guy in the bad coat." I looked down at my tweed coat, and realized that it had become wrinkled. At least she didn't say "next to the fat guy in the tie."

"Describe him," Margaret said cruelly.

"He's the tall funny looking red-haired man. I'm sure I'm not going to forget him. There's not a whole lot of people who look like him."

"Except Tom Bottoms," my client loudly whispered to me. The judge scowled but said nothing. I'm not sure the jury heard anything, as the prosecutor is usually seated next to the jury. We were at least forty feet from the jury box.

Margaret showed the teller some of the bank's photos and she identified them as being taken by the bank's security camera, over my objection. My cross was so perfunctory that the jury barely noticed I'd stood up.

The clock hit 4:45 when the teller left the witness stand, so the judge adjourned the case for the day. Instead of asking us to come back on Monday, however, she ordered us back in at 9 a.m. on Friday.

"I'm not taking this case into next week," she said darkly. "Do you think we'll finish tomorrow, Madame Prosecutor?"

"I only have one more witness, the victim."

"And you, counsel, who are you calling for the defense?"

"Not sure yet," I said. I hadn't decided whether to let my client take the stand. There was no other witness.

"So if your mystery witness takes the stand, are we still going to close tomorrow?" the judge asked impatiently.

"Probably."

"Okay, let me rephrase the question. No matter who takes the stand, we *are* going to finish this case, including closing, tomorrow. Am I understood?"

I could have protested that you can't rush justice, but this judge was famous for doing just that. I nodded.

"I'll do my best, your honor."

The next morning the jury was in the box exactly at 9 a.m. and Margaret called the client's father. He was a small, round man with a perpetually worried expression. He was one of those bald men who comb their few strands of hair across their head. He wore a casual blue shirt and neatly pressed gray slacks. He did not seem evil at all, merely sad and confused and under too much stress.

"My son has never been right since he came home from Vietnam," he said. "I don't know what happened to him over there. He told me he'd been Agent Oranged, but I'm not sure about anything he tells me."

"Objection."

"Overruled. Ask your next question, counsel."

Margaret took Farmer Senior through the whole sad scenario.

My client had come home some years ago after staying in a VA hospital in Long Beach for a while. He would sometimes re-live the war in the living room, piling all of the cushions from the couch and chairs into the middle and hiding behind it. Because Farmer Senior had wisely removed all firearms from the house, all that my client could use as weaponry was a broomstick. All of this came in without objection from me. I knew it was actually making my client seem like a sad, rather pathetic case. It was also negating the intent to steal, an element of the crime the DA had to prove to convict him. I'm not sure what Margaret thought she was going to accomplish. I didn't dare ask her.

"Did you give him permission to use your bank account?"

"No. He took the passbook without me knowing."

"Do you love your son?"

The man bowed his head. His face tightened. He was fighting off tears.

"Yes," he said in a low voice.

"If he had taken your savings, would that have been with your permission?"

"No."

"No more questions."

As I stood up, the judge leaned forward.

"Mr. Farmer, do you want to take a break before the Public Defender begins cross examination?"

"No. I want to get this over with."

The judge shrugged and gestured toward me.

"Your witness, counsel."

I asked him a few more questions about his son's strange behavior and elicited that Farmer *fils* had been accusing his father of stealing his checks. Margaret allowed this in without objection, to my surprise. It could prove my client's belief he had a legitimate claim on the money in the bank account, and so not guilty of theft.

But when I stole a few glances at the jury and saw that their stony expressions had not changed toward my client, I realized they were not buying any defense today. If anything, most of them seemed angry that we had decided to go to trial and put the poor father through this agony. I had nothing to lose.

"Mr. Farmer, do you know someone named Tom Bottoms?"

There was a long silence. He looked at me as if I'd slapped him in the face. His potato nose was squished up. I'd seen that look before on a witness: It meant you'd hit them somewhere unexpected. He looked around to the judge and the DA, hoping someone would say something. No one did.

"Tom Bottoms?" he said weakly.

"Do you know someone named Tom Bottoms?" I repeated, my blood running fast.

"Yes."

"He looks just like your son, doesn't he?"

Another long silence, as the father looked to the son.

"Yes. Except Tom's a little shorter."

"It's been a family joke for years that they are illegitimate twins, isn't it?"

"Yes."

"Where is Tom Bottoms now?"

"I don't know."

"Could it have been Tom Bottoms in the photos from the bank, and not my client?"

"Objection, speculation," Margaret said, finally catching on to what was happening.

"Sustained on foundation grounds. Mr. Farmer," the judge said, leaning toward the father, "have you seen the photos of the alleged bank transaction?"

"No."

I could have shown the photos to Farmer Senior while he was in the box. But that was a gamble. What if he looked at them and said they weren't Tom Bottoms? Better to let the jury wonder. That, after all, was reasonable doubt.

"Continue your questions, counsel," the judge prodded.

"What about the checks he said you stole from him?" I asked. Hey, why not ask?

"No, those only exist in my son's imagination."

"Thanks, nothing further."

I sat down with conflicting emotions. On one hand I was pleasantly stunned by the revelation that Tom Bottoms did exist. On the other, I wanted to go back and strangle the investigator who hadn't bothered to try to track the man down.

As I sat down my client was glowing like a comet. "Good job," he said. "I told you I was innocent."

But Margaret was having none of it. My hurried, whispered request that she dismiss the case was answered by a little snort. So when Margaret finished her evidence and closed her case, I asked for a recess so that I could make "a motion." The jury was excused until Monday. They groaned at the thought of coming back, but they left without starting a riot. Barely.

After lunch I came back into the courtroom to find my client sitting at counsel table uncuffed. Because of his unpredictable nature, the bailiffs had been discreetly handcuffing him to the chair, covering the cuffs with his shirt sleeve.

"Counsel, you have a motion," the judge said dryly. My heart began to pound. Was the judge about to grant my motion to dismiss?

"Yes, your honor," I said in a quavering voice. "Seems to me that the father has injected enough reasonable doubt into this case to take it out of the hands of the jury. The people have failed to prove their case beyond a reasonable doubt. I move for dismissal under Penal Code Section 1118."

The judge regarded me closely for a full minute. Then she turned to the D.A.

"Madame Prosecutor?"

"We've proven the case. This Tom Bottoms character is a figment of the imagination. It doesn't rise to the level of reasonable doubt..." and she went on that way for about ten minutes, uninterrupted by myself or the judge. It was a measure of how desperate she was. Her usual response to my dismissal motion is to snort and give a one-liner. When she had wound herself down, the judge turned back to me.

"Anything else, counsel?"

"Tell her I'm innocent," the client said, pleading.

"No, thank you, your honor."

"Well, I think you've made some good points, counsel," she said looking at me, "But I can't quite see my way to dismissing this case. I will, however, release your client on his own recognizance. If I do that, Mr. Farmer, will you make sure to come back Monday morning?"

"You bet, your honor."

"Fine. Mr. Farmer is released on his own recognizance and is ordered to show up in this department at 9 a.m. Monday. Sharp. You hear that, Mr. Farmer?"

"Loud and clear, your honor."

"Have a good weekend everybody."

I was glad that I wasn't Margaret's boyfriend that weekend. She must've felt the case slipping away from her, and this makes a prosecutor surly. I, on the other hand, slept about two hours. There was a chance I could win this impossible case. If I did so, my career with the office would take off.

On Monday morning we were all there at 9 a.m.—except Farmer. The jury sat in the box looking around. The judge glanced at her watch. The D.A. tapped her feet and tried not to look too pleased. At 9:30 the judge finally called us up to the bench.

"Looks like I was an idiot to grant that O.R.," she said. "Are either of you prepared to go forward without Mr. Farmer?"

"Can we do that?" I asked.

"Sure. It's a misdemeanor and you can waive your client's presence. Or if that makes you queasy—and I see by the look on your face that it does—then I can rule that the client has purposely absented himself from the proceedings and order the trial to go on without him. There's case law that says I can do that, counsel, so don't get into a huff."

"It makes me nervous," I said.

"As well it should. Do you have other witnesses for the defense?"

"No, your honor."

"Then we should think about final arguments."

As she said this, the door swung open and Farmer ran in as if pursued by the furies. He sat at my table quickly, the wind still whirling around him. The judge looked up, was momentarily surprised, then viewed the man with narrowed eyes.

"Mr. Farmer, you're late."

"Sorry, your honor, they just let me out this morning and there was no bus from the jail to here."

There, he'd said it. He had been in jail. Now the jury knew, too.

"They didn't let you out until this morning?"

"Something about a warrant for a traffic ticket. This morning they said the warrant was recalled. I had to walk all the way here, and I'm very tired."

"You should be. That's a twenty mile walk."

I walked back to the counsel table, then almost came to a dead stop. They had released him in the clothing he'd been arrested in: The mesh shirt, the parachute pants. The same ones worn in the bank photos. This was worse than having the jury see him handcuffed.

I sat down beside him and whispered: "Don't you have any other clothes?"

"Not right now."

"Great," I said.

"Call your first witness," the judge said.

"We call Darren Farmer." What else could I have done?

He looked appropriately solemn when taking the oath. I kept hoping that the jury wouldn't notice the mesh shirt and parachute pants. When I snuck a look at them, they were all earnestly looking at Farmer as if he were the newest exotic fish in the aquarium.

Carefully, I took him through the minefield of the case. Where had he been on the afternoon in question? Looking for a job. He was a Vietnam vet, he said, and finding jobs wasn't easy. Everyone looked at you like you were a trained killer who might go off at any second. Was it he who had tried to cash in his father's savings account? No, that was obviously Tom Bottoms, who looked a lot like him. During the entire direct examination, I held my breath. Yet never once did he mention Linda Ronstadt.

When I had finished with him, I sat and allowed myself a second to exhale. But I knew that Margaret would not let him slip away so easily.

She approached him with the bank picture in her hand.

"Does this man in the photo look familiar?" she asked archly.

"Of course. That's Tom Bottoms."

"And does Tom Bottoms have a mesh shirt and parachute pants similar to those you're wearing right now?"

"He likes to dress just like me to increase the confusion. You can get these clothes all over the place."

"And does Tom Bottoms have this scar on his left cheek, just as you do?"

"I don't know. I haven't seen him lately."

"Do you see the scar in the photo here?"

"No, I don't."

"Your father said that Tom Bottoms was not as tall as you are. Is that true?"

"He's about half a foot shorter."

"The man in the photo seems to be pretty tall."

"Bad angle of the photo, I guess."

"Why do you think Tom Bottoms would try to frame you for this crime?"

"Objection," I jumped up. "Speculation."

"It is speculation, but I'm going to allow him to answer the question." The judge was as fascinated as the rest of us. "You may answer, sir."

"I think it's because he and my father want to share in my earnings. I have my checks sent to the house, and I think my father and Tom Bottoms are trying to keep it for themselves."

Margaret smiled and walked back to her desk. It suddenly occurred to me that she had no idea of his Linda Ronstadt fixation. She didn't bother to ask the obvious follow-up question: *Earnings from what?* I suppose she thought he was referring to some kind of veterans' benefits.

"No further questions," she said to my surprise.

"I have nothing further," I said, hastily. Farmer came back

down from the witness stand smiling triumphantly. He had done well, better than some of my clients who were sane. Perhaps a little madness made you a better witness.

We wrestled over jury instructions for the rest of the morning, out of the presence of the jury. I wanted an instruction saying that defendant's honest but mistaken belief in his right to the money in the account obviated the intent to steal, but the judge denied me, saying that the client had not said he didn't intend to steal, he'd said that he wasn't there at all. Farmer nodded at this, as if the judge had discerned a deep and subtle truth which his idiot lawyer had somehow charged past.

In final argument, Margaret gave my client withering looks as she pointed at the photos again and again. At one point she walked near my client and held up the photo next to his face. "Look familiar?" she said. She was angry with my client for having done so well on the stand, for making her job harder. Her anger just accentuated her dark eyes and high cheekbones. During a particularly scathing portion of her argument, in which she stated that my client was an excellent actor on the witness stand and should get an Oscar for his testimony, Farmer leaned over to me.

"She's pretty good looking," he said.

"Hmm," I said noncommittally. When we were in trial, I stopped looking at her as a woman.

"Do you think she'd like to go have a cup of coffee with me when this case is over?" Farmer said. I looked at him, searching for a trace of irony in his expression. He was rapt watching her.

"Only if it's in the Main Jail mess hall," I said.

For my part, I kept my argument short. I noted that Tom Bottoms was still out there and that it could have been him. I picked up the bank photo and saw, as if for the first time, that it was blurry. "Is this enough for reasonable doubt? I can't even make out the features of the guy at the counter, can you? This is really no evidence at all." I surprised myself by actually believing it.

The judge droned the instructions and Farmer continued to gaze longingly at Margaret. To amuse myself during the crushing boredom of the instructions, I imagined Farmer wooing and winning the lovely Margaret. They would make a home together somewhere in the suburbs. She'd go to work every day and he'd sit at home waiting for his royalty checks from Linda Ronstadt. When she got home they'd have a big fight over something they saw on television, then they'd go into the bedroom and have wild uncompromising sex, the kind that makes the wallpaper come off. Afterward, they'd relax with a cup of coffee.

I roused myself just in time to hear the judge send the jury out.

"Counsel, please stay behind after the jury's out of the room," she said, arching her brow at me. We waited for the jury to exit. Then the judge shuffled papers in front of her, not looking at them at all. She fixed me with a gaze, part ironic, part disapproving. Judges like to blame public defenders for every crazy thing that happens in their courtroom.

"I'm worried that when the jury comes back with a verdict, we won't be able to find your client," she said to me.

"He's here now, your honor," I said. Secretly, I was hoping she'd put him back into custody so that *I* knew where he was. But I wasn't about to say this out loud. I hoped that she would divine it. She smiled at me.

"I could take him into custody again. Would that make you happy?"

My client shook his head.

"Well, then, counsel, he's your responsibility. Make sure you don't lose sight of him before the jury comes back." With that she left the bench.

He looked over at me. It was a little before noon.

"What's for lunch?" he said.

For the next few hours, Darren Farmer followed me around the courthouse like a lovesick puppy. I bought him a sandwich from the lunch truck downstairs. We sat outside and ate. Farmer eyed every woman who walked by as if she was basted with barbecue sauce.

"She's very good looking," he would say. "Do you think she'll go out to have a cup of coffee with me?"

We wandered the halls of the courthouse as I tried to catch up on my other misdemeanor cases. I told him to sit in the back of the calendar court, then checked up on him every ten minutes like one would a five-year-old. When I finished my last pretrial, I went back to talk to him. He wanted to know if the court reporter might want to have coffee with him sometime. Since she was married to a six foot six bailiff, I hazarded the guess that this was not going to happen.

Every six minutes he would ask, "Is the jury back yet?"

"Since they haven't called me, I doubt it," I said the first time.

"So they'll call you?"

"Yes, the courthouse is not that big."

The twelfth time he asked "Is the jury back yet?" I snapped.

"Are we in the courtroom?"

"No."

"Do you see me taking a verdict?"

"No."

"Then the damned jury isn't back yet."

"Just asking," he moped. Six minutes later, he asked the same question again—right after wondering aloud whether a young woman with a baby at her breast might be interested in going with him for some coffee.

It took three hours for that jury to decide the case, three of the longest hours I've spent in a courthouse. My six foot red-haired shadow followed my every step, happy to have someone in his life who had to answer questions for him, even the same question asked over and over. It occurred to me at hour two and three quarters that his constant asking about the jury was his feeble attempt to make conversation. Since the testimony was done and he'd had his day in court, he had nothing else to talk about. I thought, briefly, of asking him about his time in Vietnam. But who knows what torrent this would have released. So I kept quiet.

About three-thirty, the bailiff found us sitting in an alcove, watching the girls go by and speculating which of them would have coffee with either of us.

"The jury's back," he said.

My client stiffened. Up until now, the concept of a verdict was just that—a figment of his imagination, like his royalty checks from Linda Ronstadt and his success with the ladies over coffee. Now, suddenly, it was a part of reality, and a queasy one at that. He stood up and walked into the courtroom as if under remote control.

The jury filed slowly back into the box. You can usually tell what a verdict is by the way the jury comes back into the box. If they are jovial and smile at you, it's likely that you've won. If they avoid your eyes, it's because they're embarrassed that your client has been found guilty.

The jury snuck into the box that day. They looked at the floor and found their seats as quickly as they could. They stared at the judge as if she was the most interesting person they'd ever seen. No one glanced at the defense table.

I thought about leaning over and telling Farmer that I didn't like the looks of this, but then I saw his face: It was stony. He'd figured it out himself.

"Has the jury reached their verdict?" the Judge asked.

"We have, your honor," said a grim-faced elderly man, who stood with the verdict form. It floated from his hand, to the bailiff's, to the clerk. The clerk stood and read in a bland voice:

"The People of the State of California versus Darren Farmer.

We the jury in the above-entitled action find the defendant, Darren Farmer, guilty of the charge of violating Section 487(a) of the Penal Code, Grand Theft."

"Do you want the jury to be polled?" the Judge said to me. Usually I will; it gives that one holdout the last chance to change his or her mind. But that line of sad and set faces was not going to change its mind about anything. And this was no time to make the judge even more frustrated than she already was. She would, after all, have to sentence my client next.

"No, thank you, your honor."

Margaret sat smiling. She folded her arms and faced me with that little cruel, triumphant expression on her face that made me glad I'd never even slightly felt romantically inclined toward her. The judge said a few nice things to the jury about how important they were and the lawyers would like to talk to them, if they wished, when all this was done. Then she discharged them. They cleared the room as if it was filled with a noxious gas, and I never saw a one of them again.

"Well, counsel, your client has a right to be sentenced no less than five hours or more than twenty days from now. Does your client wish to be heard?"

I thought certainly that Darren Farmer would want to take the stand again, to beg and plead and rage against this travesty of justice. But he merely shook his head and said, in a low voice, "I want to get out of here. I don't want to come back to court."

"No, your honor," I said. "We're ready for sentencing now."

"Your honor, I wish to be heard," Margaret jumped up, her expression boiling. "I think this man needs to be locked up and put on formal probation. I think he needs to do a year in jail and get some psychiatric help. Otherwise, he'll be back."

"Your comments are noted. What about the defense?"

I looked at Farmer. This was the perfect chance for him to stand up, to tell her he was innocent, to say that it was all a mistake and he wanted an appeal. It certainly would have been in character. But he sat like he was carved into the chair. The change in him was frightening. I wondered whether he would get violent. I recalled the story of him fighting the war in his father's living room. Nervously, I looked around the room for a broom handle.

"Mr. Farmer," I said, "the judge wants to know if you want to tell her anything before she sentences you?"

I expected anything but silence. Silence, however, is what I got. I stood.

"Your honor, I think my client needs time to adjust to this—"

"No," he said quickly. "I don't want to come back to court.

185

Let's get it over with. Now. Whatever she wants to give me. Just get it done."

"It could be a year," I whispered to him.

"Now," he said. Then folded his arms. He was no longer in the mood to play.

"Your honor, my client asks for immediate sentencing."

"Do you want to say anything before I pass sentence?" she said, giving nothing away. I looked at her face, then to my client's. I shrugged.

"Fine," she said, writing in the file. "Counsel, how long was your client in custody?"

"Thirty days, your honor."

"Mr. Farmer," she continued, "you're sentenced to 90 days in the county jail. You have credit for thirty days plus fifteen days good time, work time. You are remanded into the custody of the sheriff forthwith. You are also ordered to do three years of informal probation. One hundred dollars to the state restitution fund. Stay out of trouble, Mr. Farmer. Next time I see you in here, I *will* give you a year. We're done here." She folded the file and flew off the bench.

I looked at Farmer. He was still sitting there, not quite quivering. I wondered whether he was going to cry.

"Do you want to appeal?" I had to ask this for every case.

"No. I just want to get back to the jail," he said tightly. The bailiff came over and put the cuffs back on him. He disappeared behind the courtroom and went down to the tank. I never saw the man again.

Margaret paced back and forth. She was furious.

"How could she give him ninety days? That was the pretrial offer! Why make a pretrial offer if you're just going to give the guy the same amount of time after trial? And that guy's nuts. He needs to be on formal probation."

"Margaret, let it go."

She stopped and looked at me. I think she forgot I was even in the room.

"This doesn't make sense," she said. "I'm not sure what I want to do now."

I packed up my briefcase. She was standing next to the table looking lost. She glanced at the blurry photos in her hands. She seemed very small. And almost human.

"Tell you what," I said, "let's go get a cup of coffee."

Acknowledgements

Pieces in this book have previously appeared in the following publications:

Valley Lawyer

Lawyer's World

Orange County Lawyer

Legal Studies Review

State Bar of California New Lawyer Training

About the Author

M.C. Bruce has been practicing law since 1987. As the old joke goes, someday all that practice will pay off.

After a four-year tour (1974-78) in the U.S. Air Force (during which he seved in Turkey and Italy), he graduated from Humboldt State University with his B.A. in Journalism in 1984, winning the Bret Harte Award for highest grade average in the graduating class. This did not impress either his professors or his fellow journalists. Then, foolishly, instead of parlaying that stunning accomplishment (he graduated Magna Cum Laude) into a glittering career as a celebrity journalist, he threw it all away by going to law school.

UC Berkeley's Boalt Hall School of Law begrudgingly acknowledges him as an alumni, but they are usually quick to add that he was not on the law review, did not graduate with honors and, as far as they are concerned, is one of the least interesting of that storied school's graduates. Sadly, they are right.

Mr. Bruce's career includes two different stints working for the Orange County Public Defender's Office in California, during which he handled misdemeanors, felonies, mental health cases and juvenile cases. They couldn't figure out where to put him until he landed in Major Frauds and they realized that this was the perfect place to hide the unwanted step child. He handled those cases for five glorious years.

He first left the OCPD in 1989 to work for a major L.A. Law Firm, but was laid off when the firm spun out of control. The firm eventually dissolved but Bruce insists he had nothing to do with the firm's demise. Investigation is ongoing.

He also practiced five years solo in Los Angeles, during which time he wrote allegedly funny columns for the San Fernando Valley Bar Association's lawyer's magazines. He was so popular that he was elected a board member of the SFVBA—but never served a day, as he was re-hired in Orange County in 1995. He worked at the OCPD the second time for 13 years. During that time he continued to write supposedly funny columns and articles for the Orange County Bar Association's magazine.

He left to head the Humboldt County Alternate Defense Council's Office but lasted less than a year at that job. He went solo in 2007.

Mr. Bruce has been published as a poet as well. His chapbook *Clients* sold out twice. An expanded edition will soon be available as an e-book and an on-demand print book.

Mr. Bruce has one child, a son who is far smarter than he is. The boy graduated from UC Berkeley in Physics and Math with honors. The child has vowed never to waste his marvelous brain in practicing law. There is hope for the younger generation after all.

Meanwhile...damn, this is a long bio...Mr. Bruce worked for a year as the Family Law Facilitator in Del Norte County and is presently on the appointed counsel list for criminal cases.

He is available for parties and bar mitzvahs and the occasional Order to Show Cause.

www.ingramcontent.com/pod-product-compliance
Lightning Source LLC
Chambersburg PA
CBHW032006170526
45157CB00002B/568